On Path

SHERRIE LARYSE

SHERRIE LARYSE
www.sherrie.com.au

Cover Design: Cheryl Read

Copyright © 2023 Sherrie Laryse

All rights reserved. No part of this publication may be reproduced in any form or by any means, electronic or mechanical, including photocopying, recording, or by any information storage and retrieval system, without the prior written permission of the author, except in the case of brief excerpts used in critical articles and reviews, and certain other noncommercial uses permitted by copyright law.

Some of the names mentioned in this book have been changed to protect the privacy of individuals.

Disclaimer:
This is an individual publication, not sponsored, endorsed or connected with the LEGO Group.
®2021 The LEGO Group. LEGO is a trademark of the LEGO Group.

for you

Contents

Introduction	1
The Challenge	8
Violins	15
Back on Track	17
Wavering	20
Legacy	27
Meeting Lucy	34
The Next Goal	41
I'm Fine.	50
The Art of Conversation	58
The Finger & The Party	67
Symptoms Are Just the Messengers	72
Connecting Dots	80
Queen Bee	89
Samatha and Vipassana	93
Mother's Day	97
Update	102
Meditation and Death	103
Game of Lego	107
Lego Practice	111
The Shift	114

Vantage Point	117
Beyond Purpose	121
Mindset	124
Wendy	128
Being Whole	133
Love	139
The Dance Floor	146
Two Lumpy Messengers	150
Wendy's Funny Game	155
Attachment	160
As Above, So Below	164
Perfect As We Are	169
Thinking	171
Undressing Wendy	178
My Consummate Teacher	185
Act Four, Scene Three	189
Tapping In	193
Post Retreat Flow	197
Act Four, Scene Three, Frame 22	204
Full Circle	210
On Path	213
The End	219
With Gratitude...	224

Introduction

It was October 2008. I was thirty years old. A friend invited me along to a weekend introductory training course that sounded interesting—mind stuff. It was right up my alley. Our trainer for the weekend, Chris, wore a shiny blue suit, and not a hair on his head was out of place. He owned the stage. He spoke at such a fast pace and with such excitement that it was as if the information he shared was bigger than his stocky body could contain as he strode across the stage. Every now and again he'd pause, becoming still and momentarily silent. He'd take a deep breath in, the air inflating him upright to hold a taller stance. His face would grow soft and sincere, as if he were about to deliver life-changing news. His speech slowed and his volume dropped as he affirmed to us just how powerful the human mind really is. The confidence with which he relayed this notion had me captivated. I drank it all in. He unpacked the human experience like it was something we could remodel and shape according to our desires. *Do we really have that much capacity to impact our experience?* I was willing to explore what he had to say.

On Sunday evening, after two very full days, Chris sent us home to apply what we'd learned. The level of enthusiasm in his voice almost ruptured his composure as he delivered the homework.

> "I want you to set yourself a *huge* goal. Create, for yourself, a goal so big, so enormous, so grandiose, that when you achieve it, you will know for certain that it was *only* as a result of what you learned here this weekend."

I left the Convention Centre with my insides buzzing. On the ferry home that night, the spring air was so cool that ordinarily I would have gone inside to sit down. That night, though, I wanted to feel a breeze that matched the force of the fire building within me. From my seat outside, I watched Sydney's city lights grow distant as the ferry moved toward Manly, those twinkling coloured lights representing all that this city had just offered me—the opportunity to rethink my thinking. Where I would take this new theory of mind was up to me now.

A grandiose goal, he said . . . The over-achiever within baited me to go beyond just *one* goal. Why stop at one? The fire in me had been lit. If I was going to do this work anyway, there were actually three things I desired: I wanted out of the corporate job that I'd grown to dislike, I wanted $50,000 cash for a house deposit, and I wanted to meet my future husband. There and then, that's what I wanted. And, at that exact moment, in that positive mindset, it all seemed perfectly achievable.

The next day, on my lunch break, I took myself downstairs to the bland, yet convenient café. I found a quiet table away from my colleagues where I could sit alone with my pen and paper. I had goals to work on. I conjured up a plan which appealed to two out of my three goals. I called my mum and announced that a redundancy was the obvious solution.

"Hmmmm . . ." She wasn't as thrilled about my plan as I was.

At two o'clock, I headed back up to my desk, logged onto my computer, and saw a meeting request from the Managing Director. Fronting up at his office a minute ahead of schedule, I noticed that he didn't look as sharp as Chris, my weekend trainer. The red tie offsetting his black suit white shirt combination was the only excitement in this over-sized office, which was otherwise devoid of colour. There was a distinct lack of enthusiasm in his voice, and I wondered whether he would choose to be here if he had another option.

"Sherrie, please take a seat." He proceeded to tell me that I was looking uninspired in my current position and offered me a new (yet utterly undesirable) role within the company.

"Danny, I fucking hate my job." This black and white, unplanned statement fell out of a mouth that was apparently unattached to keeping my employment. I had loved my job when the company was owned by my previous boss. Since the takeover though, there was a joke around the office that you had to get an approval form signed off every time you wanted to pee. The red tape transformed my well-oiled department into a sluggish old workhorse. Yet even the workhorse was more appealing than the offer he'd just put on the table.

> "I'm a people-person. I have a team of one hundred staff. It's true that I've become uninspired in this role; however, you suggesting I remove myself from my department to write an operations manual is like putting me in solitary confinement. Thank you, but I can't."

My lunchtime thoughts hung there in front of me like dangling carrots, and every word I heard him say after that was internally translated into an opportunity for me to be made redundant. With my imagined new version of reality as the only way forward, I declined the new role and we both tiptoed around the 'R' topic without either of us saying the word. The meeting was adjourned to Friday allowing both of us time to "think about it".

Think about it, I did. I applied everything I'd learned. I focused on the $50,000 goal and was proud of myself when I thought to tweak it to be *$50,000 or more.*

Friday's meeting arrived. Black suit. White shirt. *Blue* tie. Wild . . . My boredom for corporate life had officially peaked. And then, the coveted redundancy was laid out on the table. My facial muscles worked overtime to stifle what would have been an enormous grin. *Maintain composure.* I put on my best poker face, held back my insides from screeching with joy and then politely accepted my redundancy payout of $50,132. *$50,000 or more . . .* I was laughing so hard on the inside it would have definitely been accompanied by snorting if I had let it out. I was part bemused, part impressed, part inspired and utterly excited.

A good friend, Cameron, lived upstairs from me and I raced the news up to him as soon as I arrived home. We agreed that this was cause for celebration. The local Jazz Festival was on that coming weekend, so we invited our respective friends around for a big barbecue breakfast on our communal back deck, with live jazz to follow. It rained on the day, and so breakfast was moved indoors to my apartment. As people were arriving, a guy with long curly hair in a light-blue tie-dyed T-shirt knocked on my door.

"Hi, I'm Joel. I'm Cameron's friend."

One year later, Joel proposed.

It was the beginning for me—of a lot of things . . . life as I know it. Not just my life*style*, but *life*. I was doing it. Three 'grandiose goals' in one week. I was out of my job. I had $50,000 cash. I had met my husband.

Everything came under question from that point forward. Human life. The human experience, and what we are truly capable of. There is nothing within me that thinks this series of events was coincidental.

French philosopher Pierre Teilhard de Chardin once wrote, "We are not human beings having a spiritual experience; we are spiritual beings having a human experience." Whichever way we choose to see it, every part of me knows that we are more than just meat, electrical impulses, and chemistry. We have the capacity to fulfil our grandest goals. We have the capacity to create our journey.

This book tells the story of my personal investigation into what this journey is all about—what life is. What is behind it all? Do we have control over every aspect of our lives, or just some aspects? And is this level of control ever-present, or only when we're feeling powerful, such as when we're especially inflated after a weekend rah-rah seminar? Or is it about congruence? What if our superficial *wants* misalign with our deeper, more authentic desires? Who wins that rally? If we apply the same techniques which allowed me to secure three *wants* in one week, will these techniques always influence our environment in our favour, or only if the wanted outcome is aligned with our most authentic desires?

This book shares my lived experience of seeking the answer to these questions. The unanswered questions ran my life. Life took a few turns along the way and my thinking expanded with each new turning point. I journalled at each turn. I wrote through my realisations. Each of these realisations, like cookie crumbs, led me to the next stage. This book is merely the product of following those cookie crumbs. They kept me writing until I reached the point of recognising perfection in life. All of life. Perfection in each of us, individually and collectively, just the way we are. This is what I want to share with you.

The Challenge

In July 2012, Joel and I agree it's time to start a family. It's a conversation that has been tabled several times over the last couple of years. Previously, my eagerness to start a family exceeded Joel's. Something's changed though. He arrives home after a two-week surf trip in the Maldives, opens the front door and drops his bags. Having missed each other's touch, we just stand there in the doorway, holding each other in close. Without much fanfare, he looks at me and says, "Okay, let's do it. Let's have a baby." I have no words, only a smile for him. Our eyes remained locked. I'm sure mine light up. The thought of starting a family instantly gives me butterflies in my stomach.

A few months in, I begin applying all the techniques I'd learned at Chris's weekend training in how to achieve my goals. I remember how to play this game. I write down what I want, writing it in the present tense as if it's already true; "I *am* a mother". I imagine this goal as fulfilled, visualising all the detail of what life looks like when this is my reality. I visualise our home, our baby's room, Joel's facial expressions as he holds his own child. I visualise my parents' facial expressions when I introduce them to their grandchild. I tune into the whole sensory experience of this desired future, imagining what it sounds, smells, and feels like to be a mum.

After a few more months, I proceed to swallow hundreds of prenatal supplements, and put myself on a cardio regime.

More months pass by, and I include acupuncture, massage, and Chinese herbs in my protocol.

Time continues to pass. I start "Yoga for Fertility" classes, and hypnosis sessions.

Still with an empty womb, I make an appointment to see a homeopath. I fill out her four-page questionnaire on my health and score an A+. This is ironically disappointing. We need to find the *problem*. Why am I not falling pregnant? I swallow flower and herbal essences, and we tweak the tincture at each session in response to my body's changes. The homeopath is expecting me to announce success upon arrival to each new appointment. Statistically, if your body responds positively to homeopathy for fertility, pregnancy generally occurs within three or four months. After this time, the rate of success plummets to nearly zero.

I see the homeopath for four months.

Eighteen months in, with a heart that is starting to

show signs of emotional strain, Joel and I visit the IVF clinic to ensure nothing is fundamentally "wrong" with either of us. Medical checks are completed, and we are given the thumbs up, assured that all the necessary bits are in perfect working order. The doctor suggests we give ourselves another six months of trying naturally, and if I'm not pregnant by July 2014, then we can start IVF. *A deadline. Gulp.* I'm suddenly aware of my heart beating. The pressure is on.

I start acupuncture again and book craniosacral sessions. I see a counsellor to make sure there are no subconscious blocks about becoming a mother or parenting a child with my husband—the whole bag.

In January 2014, I am ushered into a sterile room with fluorescent white lights, white walls and a white-gowned doctor who conducts an internal procedure to essentially flush the tubes to ensure they're functioning optimally. This procedure is known to stimulate the right things in the right order, and many women fall pregnant in the following month as a result.

In March I'm late. It's just as they said. Butterflies again . . . I'm getting excited. I refuse to do a pregnancy test though, because I've found it too upsetting when the result is negative. If I'm not pregnant, I'm not. But to be told by a piece of plastic when it only produces one little pink line that I can't do the thing most natural to all living creatures . . . being told by plastic that I'm incapable of procreating . . . it's belittling. *Fuck you, plastic.* I'm not doing a test. I wait with anticipation and refuse to let any urine-soaked plastic stick dictate my emotional state.

Two weeks late, and I'm standing in the cash register queue buying a new kettle when I get an awful pain that brings with it my period. The pain is intense, and I'll never know whether this is purely the train speeding in after being two weeks late, or it is a miscarriage. I like to think of it as a miscarriage, because this proves that I can fall pregnant. If I've done it once, I can do it again.

I write in my gratitude journal that I am thankful I still have the freedom to travel wherever I want, whenever I want. I can sleep all night long, and my husband and I can dine out any night of the week at a whim. I've found the positives. I'm okay.

I'm offloading with a friend one day about my pregnancy woes. She drops a bombshell that she can't have kids at all—due to past health issues. I internally kick myself. *Don't be so self-absorbed.* At the same time, in a dark place deep inside my mind, I find myself wondering if she feels comfort in certainty.

It's now May. Just for fun, Joel and I decide to have sex every single day.

July 2014 arrives. The IVF alarm bells are loud and piercing holes in my psyche.

August 2014. *Just wait one more month.* September. October.

Each month past the prescribed deadline gnaws at me more and more. I just can't make the decision to go back to the IVF clinic again. *Wait one more month.*

A beautiful woman I know says she'll pray for me. I love her for her thoughts and genuine care, but I also appreciate that this journey is mine for a reason. I am exactly where I'm meant to be and I'm on the right road. I know that, even at times when I hate it.

In late 2014, I receive an email from a well-intentioned friend who, after three years of trying to fall pregnant, opted for the IVF route and now has a little boy.

"Read this, I thought it might help."

Attached is an article about the difficulties some women experience when trying to fall pregnant. The first topic delves into all the things you have to worry about; things I've never heard of, such as the danger of over-exercising and increasing your body temperature too much for a brand-new fetus to survive. *What the—? I need to stress about that now, too? Add it to the list. Thanks for the fucking help.* The article goes on to discuss IVF and spells out my nightmares about becoming a science project and injecting chemicals into a body that I don't even put paracetamol into. It details the total mess up of your hormones and the extreme roller-coaster ride of emotions. And on top of everything else, that's before you find out that the IVF round you've just attempted wasn't successful, and you'll have to do it all over again.

I stop reading, delete the email and walk away from my computer feeling red-hot angry and filled with resentment. I am fuming that my friend would send me such a negative article. For anyone who hasn't been through IVF, it's utterly scary, and not something I would voluntarily choose to experience.

The article cycles around in my thoughts and

distracts me for days. It had summed up everything about IVF that I didn't want to deal with. I wish I felt comfortable with the concept, since so many women have had success this way. But it just goes against the grain for me. The overarching question which drives my life and decisions is about my level of control over the outcome. I need to do this myself. I rationalise my decision by telling myself that if my body isn't falling pregnant naturally, it's because something in that environment isn't baby-conducive. Something else is at play here. It doesn't make sense to me to implant a baby into an environment which isn't accepting babies right now.

By the end of 2014, I inwardly make the decision to not do IVF. I delicately air these sentiments with Joel, who is as supportive of this choice as I could ever hope for.

> "If you change your mind, at any stage, and would like to do IVF, then we'll do IVF. You just say the word. If you prefer not to, then we won't. I am just as happy to redirect our focus onto our health—and then we'll see what happens naturally. Either it happens or it doesn't, and you know that I'm happy with the outcome either way."

The dead weight of unconscious stress lifts from my whole being when I hear these words. I now recognise that stress had trailed me on this journey, starting to build up behind the curtains from about the eight-month mark. I didn't notice it building so high and wide, but it was massive.

I am happy with my new path. Instead of shoving chemicals into my body, I will go the other way and focus on becoming healthier. I will conquer perfect health.

I mentally let go of all the anger from my friend's email and feel a grounding gratitude for the breakthrough.

Violins

Along the way, it feels as though a lot of parents subtly convey the idea that not having children is like dying a slow death. If I am *choosing* not to do IVF, then, it seems this is equivalent to consciously choosing slow suicide. That being the case, I only tell three people about my new decision.

The first person I tell is my mum. She's quiet at first. She wants this baby as much as I do. After a few days, she reminds me that when she was born, her mum was forty-two. I am only thirty-seven. There's still hope. She's backing me.

Next, I call my girlfriend in New Zealand. Without the body language to match her words, I have only the sound of her voice over the phone with its deliberate, yet unconvincing, upbeat tone. She's trying hard to sound supportive, but I can hear the suicide soundtrack crooning in the background. *Change the topic. This isn't open for debate.* The decision to walk the IVF path, or not, is a highly emotional choice leading to a cascade of consequences that I cannot predict.

Lastly, over the space of about a month, I tell one more friend. He is supportive of the no-IVF decision but reminds me that it is definitely a risk and suggests that I freeze some eggs.

> "If you aren't pregnant by the time you're forty-one and want to do IVF, then thirty-seven-year-old eggs are better than forty-one-year-old eggs."

It makes perfect sense, which is exactly why it hits a raw nerve. I don't want intervention. I don't want to conceive in a sterile, fluorescent white-lit, white-walled room. I don't want to know I have eggs on ice. They're meant to be at thirty-seven-degrees Celsius living happily with their friends. They don't belong on ice. That's science and I am not a science project. My hunger to know what is possible without intervention is greater than all the logic and modern science being put forward. Despite this intrinsic drive, the suggestion of freezing eggs haunts me for a while. The crooning suicide soundtrack hums on low volume until I eventually forget about the whole egg-freezing idea—consciously at least.

Back on Track

I start a new series of guided meditations. They focus on female fertility to support a healthy womb, lots of healthy eggs, and falling pregnant. I give up coffee. For what it's worth, I remove my belly piercing with the little amethyst heart pendant that hangs in my navel. I read *Brighton Baby: A Revolutionary Organic Approach to Having an Extraordinary Child* by Roy Dittmann and apply everything the author suggests. I book myself into infrared saunas to remove toxins from my body. I buy so many powdered herbs that my morning green juices and smoothies are near disgusting. All for the greater good. I don't mind.

During the first two weeks of each cycle, I practice reflexology on myself to stimulate the key areas that I learned about during my Traditional Chinese Medicine appointments.

I sleep on a magnetic mattress and lie underneath a magnetic quilt. Magnetic Field Therapy is said to promote a deeper, more restful sleep (among other claims). Given sleep underpins optimal health, it feels worthwhile to give this a try.

I read *The Body Ecology Diet* by Donna Gates and educate myself on how health starts in the gut. I cut down gluten and cut out all refined sugars. I temporarily limit my fruit to one piece per day and I start drinking Pau D'arco and Cats Claw tea to manage candida, a yeast overgrowth common in people on a modern diet. I begin taking probiotics and making my own fermented vegetables. Joel and I modify our shopping habits to start living on predominantly organic food. I add raspberry tea to my health ritual, as it tones and supports uterine health. I learn that good gut health can be undone if you have colon issues, so I promptly arrange a colon cleanse followed by two colonics. I take chlorella and spirulina to cleanse my body of heavy metals. I enrich my blood. I increase my good gut bacteria. I start and end the day with a little lime juice or apple cider vinegar in my drinking water.

I complete an online course on "Low-Tox Living" and look at every place where there are chemicals in our home environment. I replace our "earth friendly" cleaning products with bi-carbonate soda, vinegar and eucalyptus. I use bicarb soda and peppermint oil to brush my teeth. I replace our organic shampoo with bicarb soda, and our conditioner with apple cider vinegar. I use apple cider vinegar as a fabric softener. I use clove oil, vinegar and bicarb soda to clean the shower. I am feeling liberated by the lack of chemicals in our home! The practice of clean-living spurs me on. I use less plastic and make a pact to slowly replace my plastic storage containers with glass. I buy only natural make-up and deodorants and organic cotton tampons. I buy a stainless steel water bottle. I make my own mosquito repellent from essential oils. I start researching water filters to upgrade the pretty fancy one we have already. Surely there are better filters out there and I am going to get one. Water is life.

Feeling empowered by each incremental step I've taken in my journey toward a healthier female body, I am now reaping the benefits. By February 2015, I feel and look the healthiest I have for a long while—perhaps, ever.

Wavering

In late February, Joel and I are on holiday in Cambodia. We walk along the dirt roads which are dry and dusty in this crazy-hot weather. Tucked away on the side of the street is a small roadside eatery with some plastic tables and chairs under an awning. We drop our backpacks and sit at one of the tables, happy to be in the shade. The meal portions look larger than our appetites, so we order just one chicken and rice dish with two forks. After the woman brings our food over, she very sweetly returns with a jug of iced tea and two plastic cups. We politely decline the offer; however, she says it is complimentary and leaves the cold tea for us to enjoy. While our lunch was being cooked, I had watched the ice being delivered and I saw her pay for it. We are sitting here, using her tables and chairs, sharing a meal which cost us $1.50 (Australian) and she is providing us with a free drink so we can cool down and feel more comfortable. It feels disrespectful *not* to drink it. How could I be dismissive of her generosity? My new and improved state of health lulls me into the misguided belief that I am indestructible. Against Joel's better judgement, I drink the tea made with Siem Reap's local water. My inflated confidence assures me I will be fine. Inwardly, I know exactly what I'm doing. I am testing the limits of what is possible at this level of robust physical health and mental conviction about my immunity.

The impact hits me a few hours after lunch. We about-face and head straight back to our hotel room. I lay in bed, sweating, queasy, and feeling sorry for myself. All I can do is stare aimlessly at the light-blue-grey sky through the window. My increasing feelings of nausea are compounded by feelings of regret in my gut—my stupidity for thinking I was super-human drinking that tea. *Everybody knows not to drink the water.* The thought is short-lived, quickly replaced by stronger and stronger stomach contractions which steal all of my attention. It doesn't take long before I'm alternating between vomiting and diarrhoea, both vying for first place in the race to deplete me. I continue to aggressively eject my internal contents in such rapid bouts that I actually block the hotel toilet. I'm far too exhausted to be embarrassed about it—and there's little time for that anyway. My contractions are ten to fifteen minutes apart. I need that thing cleared pronto! I manage to muster up enough energy to apologise profusely to the staff member who arrives with a plunger, heeding our call.

My gut begins to settle once everything has finally been purged. Joel leaves me alone temporarily, heading out onto the dusty streets to find someone who sells young coconuts, and brings one back for me. It's all I can keep down and the only way I can replenish my hydration and salts.

Joel's patience with me and my antics regularly floors me and has me falling in love with him even more. Sometimes I am in awe of his gentleness toward me. It's bottomless. He is my rock in all situations, bar none.

While my health stabilises enough not to ruin our holiday completely, I realise that I've also picked up some sort of bug. On returning home to Australia, tracking down this bug results in test after test, with each doctor taking turns trying to name the little critter. Now in May, after being sick for over three months, my body loses all the goodness it had built up. I have an irregular menstrual cycle, I am constantly tired, and it is pure lunacy to be too far from a toilet.

The positive side to all this is that, for a while, I forget that I'm trying to fall pregnant. The benefits of being sick! I actually wouldn't want a baby growing inside me in this state of ill health. It is a welcome distraction and a refreshing headspace to, in fact, *not* want to be pregnant.

At this point, as a thirty-seven (and a half) year old woman, I have spent three years oscillating between contrasting fundamental emotions. On average, every two months Joel holds me in close and soaks up my tears. It's despair. It's heart-sinking disappointment. It's a continuous cycle of building up and then releasing frustration. It's a deep vulnerability. It's an insatiable feeling of not being in control. And yep, there it is . . . a little bit of that slow suicide feeling and an ocean-deep sadness, longing for a little person I'll never know.

Combine this emotional turmoil with the recognition that I am in a beautiful marriage and honestly couldn't imagine being happier with any other person. We are onto such a good thing, the two of us. I've heard rumours about the pressure a new baby can put on a marriage. Why would we do that to ourselves? Maybe we don't want to. Maybe we could remain this happy until death do us part. We could choose to never share ourselves with dependents, never assign each other the role of primary carer or primary earner. Rather, we could just live a fun life the way we do now, travelling wherever and whenever we want, eating all the sashimi, salami and soft cheeses in sight—but maybe holding back next time when it comes to drinking the local water.

It's a jolting rollercoaster of a ride, emotionally and mentally. But you can't take a holiday from your head, so, I just keep looking for ways to appease it. My investigation of life and of my influence over it remains strong. I look for new approaches. I do more meditation. I find all the positives in my current lifestyle—sans children—and consider all the downsides of having children. Sometimes, that even helps.

After months of being sick from the unidentified bug I picked up in Cambodia, and test after test, a specialist finally announces that I have a particular type of colitis.

> "I've never seen this in a person your age before. Normally I only see it in elderly women."

Bang! Sore point number one. *Dear Doctor, please don't tell me that my body is responding like an elderly woman's. Elderly women don't have babies. I do. Clearly our bodies are not the same.* I should have said that. Instead, I let him continue . . .

> "We're really not sure why people get this type of colitis, but we believe it is generally stress related. Do you have something that is causing you stress?"

Doctor, you're on fire!

I walk out and crumble. Ironically, the diagnosis comes with a prescribed solution, so, realistically speaking, it is good news. It just hit a couple of raw nerves on the way through.

I take my prescribed steroids for six weeks—clearly not loving the idea but recognising I could lose more ground in my health by not fixing the problem.

The next month I am late—again. It's so unkind for your body to tease you when you're at your most vulnerable. The eventual arrival of my period is a major breaking point for me. I cry into Joel's chest like I have never cried before. Not because I'm not pregnant, but because I am glimpsing the reality of never knowing myself as a mother. Most of us grow up with a sense of knowing who we are, and I've always known myself as a mother. I know it in my bones. I now mourn the loss of the person I've always thought myself to be. Joel holds me in his lap, his arms wrapped around me. His T-shirt accepts all of my tears. My chest heaving with every breath, I begin to feel into a new reality, adopting a whole new version of myself that is different to the person I thought I was. I no longer trust who I am, or who I think I am. Losing myself is the most vulnerable feeling I've ever experienced.

I had pre-arranged to catch up with a girlfriend, and despite not wanting to leave the house, I decide to go. I know it will be beneficial for my heart and my head. As it turns out, my friend has just become qualified to teach Emotional Freedom Technique (EFT) and offers me a session. She couples EFT with 'tapping'—a whole new funky technique that I am a bit dubious about, but, at this point, I am open to anything.

I don't know whether what happened to me with EFT is commonly experienced. During the session, I go back to my childhood—to the elusive 'inner child' that wreaks havoc from within. We chat, my inner child and I, and she makes it clear that she wants to feel independent. She wants to do things on her own and to feel as if she can achieve goals unassisted. This 'chat' gives me such a sense of peace around my decision not to do IVF. When both sides of the IVF coin say, 'It's not for you, don't do it', listening to this advice seems like a sound way to make a decision with confidence. I realise that I am acting like a person who trusts themselves. I am acting like a person who knows who they are, knows themselves to the core and doesn't let any external influences cause them to waver from their life's purpose.

It's only in this moment that I realise: I've been subconsciously second-guessing my decision around IVF. I've been convincing myself intellectually that it was right, rather than feeling it in my body. Only in this moment, now, do I feel a sense of congruency around my decision to do this on our own, without IVF.

Feeling stable again, my inner pendulum balanced, tears gone, clarity regained . . . I feel strong.

The next monthly cycle around the clock and I'm not swayed by the fact that I'm not pregnant. I continue reading *The Body Ecology Diet*. I am up to the part about liver cleansing and internal cleansing. *Alright, we're on.*

Legacy

October 2015. We wake up to the aroma of fresh, home-baked bread wafting through the air. Joel prepared the bread maker last night and set the timer so the warm scent of our almost-ready loaf would be a delicious alarm clock, permeating our entire apartment. We linger in bed, being husband and wife, eventually getting up for a shower. Our rumbling bellies rush us through the morning bathroom routine, leading us directly to the source of that smell. We move around each other in the kitchen like synchronised swimmers. He cuts the bread; I lean over and smell it while igniting the gas flame under the kettle. He pulls out a couple of tea bags from the overhead cupboard and, as he lowers the tea bags, I slide the mugs in under them. I get the butter out of the fridge while he reaches for the Vegemite. There's a beautiful unspoken dance going on in our kitchen that feels like poetry.

We sit down at the table and habitually 'cheers' each other. Ordinarily, our version of cheers happens by tapping our forks together; a ritual born from not drinking alcohol together. This morning though, given cutlery isn't needed for eating Vegemite toast, we instead tap our index fingers together before taking our first bite.

The clarity of the whole routine suddenly strikes me. For the first time, I appreciate just how damned good our world is, just the way it is.

Something shifts deep within.

In mid-November, I pack my bag and head to an Airbnb apartment that I've booked on the other side of the city. I'm enrolled in a seminar, and I know the upcoming days are going to be long and full, so I want to be within walking distance of the venue. The seminar is an intensive seven days of learning with American-born polymath Dr John Demartini. In essence, he teaches about human behaviour and how to enhance all areas of your life: mental, social, relationships, career, financial, spiritual and physical.

I once heard someone say that listening to Demartini lecture is analogous to trying to drink from a fire hose. This week is no different. The fast-flowing wisdom he shares is comprehensive and seemingly endless. Every day, we guzzle knowledge for fifteen hours non-stop, pausing only for self-reflection exercises to apply the principles to our own lives.

We spend one whole day on each of the seven areas of life, with the first focused on "Mental Understanding and Wisdom." Paradoxically, our day opens with an exercise to dissolve any addiction we have to knowledge and mental acuity. This is based on the theory that anything we feel compelled to gain or retain will also create an opposing reaction within us—the fear of losing it. The exercise asks us to find the pros and cons of gaining knowledge, as well as the pros and cons of losing knowledge. By learning how to neutralise polarised views, we can live without as much emotional reaction to life's ups and downs. This results in us gaining greater stability. It allows us a greater resilience to live with purpose, less swayed by external circumstances or opinions.

The day proceeds with a fire hose drenching of physics, philosophy, neurology, cognition, and irreversibly head-expanding conversations about consciousness. This is when Demartini introduces me to my new favourite artwork, a print of a wood engraving called "The Flammarion". Although the artist is unknown, the engraving is said to be an interpretation of the human quest for knowledge. This engraving speaks directly to me and my own quest.

At the end of this mind-expanding, life-changing week, I come away with a headful of new thoughts, new realisations, new concepts and greater understanding.

There's one subject that I continue to ruminate on though: my legacy. The subject didn't come up explicitly, but all of the discussions led to this concept bubbling up in my head. The nature of my legacy is obviously something that still needs my consideration and attention.

A legacy is something that lives beyond your years. A mark you make on the world that will be remembered after you're gone. Your body may die, but the essence of your contribution lives on.

Most religions believe in some sort of life after death, and I think many of us have the desire to live beyond our body's expiry. Perhaps people hold on to the concept of immortality to soften the fear of death itself. Speaking for myself, I think my female hormones kicked in to drive my need to leave something behind, something created by me that will live on after my body is gone. It's me ticking the legacy box within.

I start to question whether the absence of a legacy is driving my yearning for a child, or the absence of a child is driving the desire to create a legacy. This quickly becomes one of those heated debates that would draw a good crowd if only it was happening outside my head. I recall the slow suicide soundtrack subliminally playing during my conversations with mothers. I realise now that when mothers commiserated with me, it was only occurring in my head. They weren't judging me. Those were *my* projections. It was *me* playing that soundtrack.

I come back to the basics. *Why do I want to be a mother?* I unpack the concept of mothering and articulate every aspect of motherhood as I define it to be. I begin listing examples of where I am already experiencing these motherly traits in my life. I keep going until I find so many examples that I truly feel I *am* fulfilling these mothering traits—over and over, again—to the same degree as I imagine I would if I were mothering my own child.

Studying with Demartini, I learn that nothing is ever missing from our lives. What we perceive to be missing will appear in another form that we're not yet acknowledging or consciously recognising. Today, I experience the truth of this wisdom. What I think is missing from my life is not actually missing. All of my needs are being fulfilled. I am already a mother, exactly in the way I define motherhood to be.

The three traits that hold the most weight for me are: *nurturing*, *mentoring* and *inspiring*. I consider how these traits play out in my life while sitting with the unanswered question of my legacy. This train of thought leads me straight into my next great internal debate.

On one side is the argument in favour of pouring all my energy into a child, into a single human. In the other corner, I argue that if I had a child of my own, it might limit my ability to help hundreds, if not thousands, of other people who I would otherwise seek to nurture, mentor and inspire in order to fulfil my mothering needs.

Would I be limiting my contribution on this planet by having my own child?

This last thought shocks me and I briskly leave the debate room, slamming the door behind me.

Later, when I tiptoe my way back to this thought, I realise that this is my legacy. I will live a life acting out my mothering characteristics by nurturing, mentoring and inspiring other people and prove to myself that nothing is missing from my world.

I drive back over the Harbour Bridge after what has been a massive week of learning. I'm thankful to have some solo time in the car to collect my thoughts before I arrive home. As soon as I walk through the front door, I speak at a million miles an hour telling Joel about what I learned from Demartini's seminar, as well as where my head went in the process. Once I've exhausted his ears, it's time for my meditation. I need to integrate all these new thoughts. I pick up my bolster and head to our bedroom. The bolster finds its usual place on the sheepskin rug, and I settle myself on top of it, getting comfortable. I slip into a beautiful meditation and visualise a future that is so inspiring to me as a life to lead, that tears run down my face. Maybe there's a baby in this picture or maybe there isn't, but the void has transformed to a point where I realise that my legacy can be just as significant as to create someone who looks like me.

Over Christmas, I let the new vision of myself linger in the background, wondering how to move forward. By February, I am homing in and make the decision that

I want to work with teenagers. Suddenly the idea of raising only my own children feels almost selfish, when there are thousands in Australia alone who could use the energy that I, as a non-parent, have to give. This decision perfectly aligns with the meditation about my future— a life path of mothering on a grand scale.

Meeting Lucy

In March, I'm back at my 'tapping' girlfriend's house for dinner. I now have the words to articulate what I want to dedicate this next chapter of my life to. My girlfriend immediately tells me about an organisation she admires that helps teenage girls who have experienced trauma. I email the organisation as soon as I arrive home after dinner.

At two o'clock the following afternoon, I receive a call from a lady named Peta who kindly explains that if I want to volunteer in the 2016 mentoring program, I will have to attend a compulsory weekend training course starting at 9:30 the next morning. If I miss this training, I will have to wait another year.

If there is such a thing as divine intervention, this was it. I cancel all my weekend plans and walk in the door of the training room the next morning at 9:10 a.m.

Peta and the rest of the team welcome me and point me towards the tea and coffee. Once all the other volunteers arrive, we sit down at a horseshoe conference table to introduce ourselves. Each of us completes a personal profiling exercise that Peta will later use to match us with one of the teenagers in the program. The trainers take us through case studies and bring us up to speed with the highly challenging environments that some of the girls have grown up in. We are provided with as much information as can be packed into one weekend to prepare us for our mentoring roles, starting in two weeks' time.

In between the training weekend and the commencement of the program, I offer to pet sit my parents' cat and dogs for a few days while they're away. My brother and his family live just around the corner, so the plan is to spend as much time with his four kids as I can. I speak with my sister-in-law and offer to pick up the boys from school, which will make it possible for her to stay home and just look after her twins. She tells me what time to be at the school and where to meet the boys, and I pull up at the school ten minutes early. As I'm walking toward the gate, a flurry of thoughts and emotions are pinballing inside me. It occurs to me that I look like all the other parents. I don't look like an aunty. I look like a mother.

I walk deliberately, through the gate and along the concrete path, as if I did this every weekday, hoping not to look lost and blow my cover. I feel a heightened sense of awareness with every step I take. *Look confident, like you know where you're going.* I watch the other parents and examine their facial expressions. Some look happy, chatting and smiling with other mums and dads. Some of them look as if this is an interruption in their day, the school run getting in the way of whatever they'd prefer to be doing. I let myself momentarily pretend that this is my everyday routine. I want to glimpse what it might feel like for school pickups to be a routine, even mundane, part of life. I walk over to the designated area and find a place where the boys will notice me as soon as they come out of their classroom. I imagine them instantly smiling when they see me, choosing me out of all the other parents.

As I stand there with an eagerness that exceeds the occasion, I see my brother walking toward me from the other gate. He got off work early and has come to surprise his boys. Seeing him—the *real* parent—instantly exposes me as a fake. My pinballs shatter on impact. I don't wait for the boys. I make it out of the school and away from all the real parents just in time; getting inside my car with the door just closing behind me before I burst into tears.

Every time I come undone, it always starts with me clawing for a glimmer of that feeling of being a parent. This was a surprise package for me, given my headspace of late. The pain feels amplified by the fact that I am away from my husband and our home and the life we've built which reassures me we're ok, just the two of us. Right now, I'm in somebody else's home—a family home—alone, while everybody else is with their families.

The reality check of this potential future as a lonely old woman smacks me down hard.

It's now April 2016. I receive details from the mentoring program about the girl I've been paired with. Her name is Lucy. As I dial her number, I feel a little nervous, as if I'm about to go on a blind date. I remind myself that I'm the mentor in this relationship. *Pull it together.* She answers the phone. My heart stops pounding and immediately opens to her. Her voice is not that of a little girl. It's smoky and captivating, it's graceful and it feels really calming. I sink deeper into my lounge as we settle in for a chat. This girl is witty. I really like her sense of humour.

After hanging up, I wonder what she thinks of me and whether I'm just 'some random woman' to her, someone she needs to be polite to and put up with during this program she's been enrolled into. Over the following days, we send a few text messages back and forth, talking about my cat, her dogs, plucking eyebrows, school . . . prolonging our conversation to build a connection. I'm feeling grounded. I feel the void filling up again.

Lucy and I exchange ongoing small talk until the day arrives when we meet in person at a four-day camp with all the mentors and the girls: 'Big Sisters' and 'Little Sisters,' as we're referred to in the program. I recognise Lucy as a version of the younger me. She's a little shy in a bigger group, yet so coolly herself when it's just the two of us. I vividly remember being sixteen. I remember the awkwardness and the confidence that comes with verging on adulthood, the new experiences, the sense of liberation as well as confinement—still not quite legal age. Perhaps that's why it feels so easy to discuss her world with her. It's like I'm just another one of her friends.

I was so hungry for this relationship, for somebody to mother, that my heart opens to love her from the moment we meet. I feel dedicated to getting to know Lucy and learning about her world. It's an honour and a humbling gift to stand by her side and offer support through this difficult phase of her life.

The first full day of camp is a combination of group activities and one-on-one time, where Lucy and I lap the oval several times while we talk. Night comes, and it occurs to me that this beautiful girl is so independent and well adjusted (at least on the surface), that I feel a little redundant in this mentoring relationship. In the middle of the night, when senses are heightened and emotions are amplified, the feeling of being unneeded swells in me as I mourn the loss of yet another opportunity to feel like a parent. I realise that it is me who desperately needs Lucy, far more than she needs me.

The next day is difficult as I battle with my feelings of loss, once again, while also attempting to put on a good front. And while I realise that *my* experience of the program is all about me, I need to reign my emotions back in for now. They need to stay subdued until I am back in the arms of my husband.

In the afternoon, Lucy opens up to me a little about some of the personal challenges she's been facing. It's a warm hug to my ears to learn that she might need me too, even if it's only as someone for her to admit things to.

Our four-day, Sister-to-sister immersion wraps up with long-sustained hugs amongst the big and little sisters. It feels like we've all known each other for years. Driving home, I already miss this new human in my life who offers me a glimpse of mothering. She feels like my access point to this sense of mothering I feel within myself. She *is* the key to what has been locked. As soon as I am home, I send Lucy a thank-you text message and reignite our back-and-forth bonding chats until our next monthly catch up.

Now that I'm in this program, I recognise that I want more. I wholeheartedly appreciate the path I'm on. I'm ready to dedicate my energy to working with people who know there's a great life out there for them if they can only figure out how to access it.

It's certainly not the case that I've turned my back on having children—not at all, not in my heart. But in the process of trying to conceive a child and moving through this challenge, I've come to realise that the challenge itself was mine to own as a part of my life education. It was a vehicle to move me from where I was to where I intuitively wanted to be, solidifying my understanding of the way I can contribute to the world.

Our challenges aren't necessarily obstacles. They can be gifts, enabling us to see bigger visions for ourselves, bigger lives, bigger contributions. They're steering devices that aim us toward our purpose. I feel that all my life experiences have accrued to prepare and qualify me for this role—if I dared to think so grandly about myself. I thought my life purpose was going to play out in having children of my own, but I now appreciate that it's so much more than that. I feel as if I just woke up to my true purpose —to work with hundreds of people who are trying to figure out their way.

I genuinely feel that I needed to be challenged in this way. I needed to transition through all the emotions I have so richly experienced to arrive at this realisation of who I am. I have both lost and found myself during this inner expedition, and I now have nothing but gratitude for every twist and turn that helped deliver me here. I truly feel that I am here to serve humanity and I now have the capacity to do so.

The Next Goal

I have tentatively set my next grandiose goal to mother ten thousand people. When I think more about it though, this number doesn't feel large enough. It would need to be an amount almost inconceivable to my mind to feel close to the magnitude of mothering my own child. It would need to be at least one million people. *Eek! Where do I even start?* That's a lot of people. But I feel if I could somehow mother one million, it might balance the scales. I need to figure out a way to nurture, inspire and mentor one million people.

I come up with the idea of giving a talk on emotional intelligence—what it is and how to attain it. I have a lot to say on this topic, thanks to amazing teachers I've had over the years. During my corporate stint, many weekends and a lot of my annual leave time was spent attending courses and trainings. I studied Ayurveda,

Human Behaviour, Psychosomatics (the mind-body connection), Neurolinguistics, Reiki, and I learned multiple meditation styles. Whenever I heard about courses which offered the opportunity to delve further into personal development, I signed up. A colleague once told me about the deep journey of self-discovery she went on as part of studying Holistic Counselling, so I enrolled at the next course intake and studied in the evenings after work.

It was the meshing of all this information which led me to start my consulting business teaching emotional intelligence to individuals. These consultations appeal to people who have either experienced emotional trauma in the past or are currently in an emotionally challenging situation. My role is to help them navigate their thinking to find new perspectives so they can feel differently about their experiences. If we alter the way we think about something, our emotions follow suit. I predominantly lean on the Demartini Method, a technique learned in one of John Demartini's trainings. This method is partly built on the philosophy of axiology—the study of values.

The results my clients achieve in those sessions continually inspire me. With me holding their hand, they work through painful memories of some of the most awful experiences, arriving at a place of relief and a whole new constructive way of thinking about themselves and their lives.

During each session, I help my clients convert their unwanted experiences into pivotal turning points in their life that are suddenly worthy of appreciation.

The qualifying question I ask them at the end of our session together is: "If you could have it any other way, would you?" When the answer comes back as 'no', I know we're done. To me, this is the attainment of emotional intelligence. Your emotional intelligence gives you the capacity to take any experience—with all the emotions wrapped up with it—and process the experience to bring yourself to equilibrium.

So, my head rolls around one question. How do I translate this information to a group environment so I can teach emotional intelligence on a grander scale? Working with clients in a one-on-one environment is one thing; delivering this information to a group is a whole new ball game. The public speaking factor rattles me a little. Not enough to prevent me from doing it, but enough that I don't wholeheartedly relax into it. It's all those faces staring at me. I pretend to look comfortable in front of them, but, in reality, I'm reading their facial expressions and trying to determine whether they like me or not. Too distracting. Is there any way to address a group of people without them looking at me?

Enter my faithful friend, yoga. In Yin yoga, people commonly practice with their eyes closed. It's the perfect vehicle. I come up with a plan to collaborate with a Yin yoga teacher. While the teacher guides students into Yin poses which they hold for several minutes at a time—importantly, with their eyes closed—I will deliver my talk, timed to fit in with each pose. It's the perfect solution. *Yinformation Sessions* are born.

After spending hours searching online to find

reputable yoga studios that offer Yin, I approach multiple teachers, introducing myself and my idea for a collaboration. Almost everyone I reach out to in Australia and New Zealand is open to the idea. After a five-week lead time to promote the first event, I begin to deliver my Yinformation Sessions at yoga studios to about twenty-five people each time. Each session opens with the yoga teacher welcoming the students, then allowing time for me to introduce myself before we begin. The light in the room is always dim. The music is soft. During the two-hour class, the students listen to the alternating voices of the yoga teacher and my own. First, the teacher explains the pose. The students follow the cues, letting their bodies become passive on their yoga mats as they close their eyes. I then deliver my talk, speaking in a slow, relaxed voice that allows all of the words to gently sink in in their own rhythm.

On one of my New Zealand tours, delivering Yinformation Sessions in multiple studios, several of the studio owners ask me whether I have a book to sell, as they have been receiving requests from their students. It's an interesting idea and my ears prick up. I like the fact that people consider the information I share to be so valuable that they want to absorb it again. This notion of writing a book someday sits quietly within me, but it's a bucket list item. It's not something I have given any serious thought to yet.

After one year of delivering Yinformation sessions and feeling more and more at home in yoga studios, I enrol in yoga teacher training myself. At first, I'm not even sure why. It just feels right. I love yoga. It seems like the fitting place to dive into next, despite not having the inclination to teach yoga myself. In my fifteen years of yoga practice, I have always been happy on the mat with someone else at the front of the class leading the way. Today, however, I make the decision to enrol, but I will sit on this decision for a few weeks before pressing the 'go' button and paying my fees. This thinking time feels necessary, mostly because the training is thousands of dollars and I'm not even sure what I'm going to do with the qualification, given I'm not planning on teaching at the other end. My heart is saying 'yes.' Yet, I prefer it when my heart and head are on the same page at the same time. My head has no idea what this is all about.

After a few weeks of consideration, my head isn't coming up with any reasons *not* to go ahead. I have the money, I have the time, I have the trust in the teacher, and I have full support from my husband. By this simple lack of a *no* response, my head defaults to *yes*.

After completing the foundational four-hundred-hour Hatha yoga training, I enrol into Yin yoga training. At the same time, I'm offered a job teaching Hatha classes at the studio where I trained. This would conveniently mean I teach Hatha in the morning, take a break for lunch and then come back for Yin training in the afternoon. I accept, and suddenly I'm a yoga teacher. This launches me into my next learning wormhole.

I can't get enough. I complete further online training with teachers whom I cannot visit in person, and I travel to those I can. Any time I'm in the car, I listen to podcasts from specialists on yoga, fascia, breathwork, the musculoskeletal system, and health in general. I weave this new knowledge into my classes to share what I've learned and make it relatable for the yogis on the mat. I am eating textbooks. Google Scholar is my new browser homepage and gives me access to all sorts of well-researched literature on the human body. I love the quote written directly below Google Scholar's search bar which states, *"Stand on the shoulders of giants"*. This is exactly what I intend to do.

By 2019, I'm at full throttle teaching yoga and loving it. The science nerd in me infuses a different flavour into the way I teach yoga. I know this style doesn't appeal to everyone, but it feels true for me and it's where I want to position myself. I've given myself a uniform of black yoga pants with either a black, navy or white singlet. Such a small thing, but it feels important. It's my way of keeping my 'look' simple, down to earth, and, hopefully, more approachable. My aim is to be relatable and thus more effective with my message—that's to say, more effective in my mothering. The uniform also helps me to anchor myself into teaching mode. I wear multi-coloured clothes when I practice on the mat as a yoga student.

My husband watches my obsession with acquiring new knowledge unfold more and more. One day, he says,

> "I think you should consider writing a book, even if it is only a small book, with all that

you've learned."

A book is beginning to feel like a project I could be ready for. Where to start, though? I look to my calendar and schedule May 2019 for dedicated time to ponder and, hopefully, birth an idea for a book.

Suddenly it's August already and well past my scheduled date. I alter my teaching schedule to allow more opportunity to teach the styles which fulfil me most. My new timetable of predominantly Yin and meditation classes allows me to tap more fully into my version of mothering. Although I love teaching Hatha yoga, there seems less space for sharing with the students, which is where I feel has the most potential for nurturing and inspiring. I'm learning to listen inward and use my predefined mothering traits as a compass for all my decisions. Albeit a few months behind schedule, this is when I get the idea to write a book about the science of yoga. The concept encompasses all I love about my yoga practice; it will include emotional intelligence, mental wellbeing, as well as the physical aspects of the yoga practice, breathwork and meditation—all backed by modern science. This feels like my book. It will highlight the science behind yoga to explain why it is such an incredibly powerful and profound practice for body, heart and mind.

In September 2019, I officially start writing. I open with the history of yoga so we can all start on the same page, figuratively and literally.

I call Mum. "I've started writing my first book."
"Good."

I'm amused that there's no surprise in her voice, nor any questions as to what it's about. Rather, there's a sense of mutual understanding that this is where I am meant to be. My maternal grandmother told me, more than once, that I was going to be a writer. I guess it was just something that my mum and I quietly and subconsciously owned as a fact that would, one day, unravel itself into reality. And so that time is now. *Good,* she says.

Now October and I already see the 'Warning: Rollercoaster Ahead' signs about writing a book. I listen to interviews and podcasts with authors doing the promotional rounds on their book tour (a prospect that makes my innards contract). Those who share their personal journey of the writing process make it sound like an epic adventure, filled with high highs and low lows. I don't know if my experience will be like that or not, but I've decided to journal about the process all the same. If I'm writing one book anyway, why not concurrently write a second book about my experience writing the first book? It is a stupid and overwhelming enough idea for the overachiever in me to feel super inspired about doing. I'm in.

And so, *this* book is born.

I'm no stranger to journalling. I spent several years writing my way through all of my experiences trying to fall pregnant. Writing was my catharsis. I wrote it all down as it happened, which means that much of the back story you've read so far had already been distilled into sentences. From this point forward, I will continue to journal my experiences, as they happen—except that from now on, I have an end goal of a book. As I write about the history, philosophy and science of yoga in the other book, I will simultaneously write this book about my personal experiences. The initial book will spell out the practical aspects of self-enquiry, while this book can be an example of that self-enquiry, using myself as the work-in-progress case study. With myself as the guinea pig, I will live the experience of my unanswered questions and share what I find along the way.

I'm Fine.

A new morning, and with my new book idea in tow, I meet up with a friend for coffee. We haven't seen each other in ages, maybe close to a year. We bypass the small talk.

"So, tell me what's going on. Lay it on the table."

She pours out all her thoughts, conundrums and emotions for a good forty minutes and I lap it up, thankful we don't have to waste time warming up in order to be there for each other. We go back and forth, weighing her experiences and determining how to best navigate them. Exhausted of words, she throws her head into her hands, peers up over her fingertips and lets out a, "So, how are you?"

"I'm fine."

"You're fine? What does that mean? Are you

okay?"

"Yes, seriously, I'm really fine. I'm great. I'm good."

I am genuinely fine. That's the problem. Since stewing on the idea of writing this more personal book, it has become obvious to me that I need to park the initial book about the science of yoga and focus solely on writing this one. This book feels enough. And yet, by putting a single, concentrated spotlight on my personal journey, I suddenly feel pressured to have a worthy back story, something with enough weight to justify writing this book and daring to think it worth sharing. I have been contemplating—and struggling with—the fact that I've always been fine. I question whether I have a book in me worth writing that will be more than just *fine*.

I consider myself an ordinary person. My life's highs and lows, while they felt turbulent at the time, seem quite ordinary to me now. I achieved a trifecta of goals in a way that I believe we all have access to. The pregnancy challenges I faced were deeply personal, and often unspoken, but common all the same. As I moved through those challenges, each new hurdle and subsequent heartache persuaded me to use my keyboard as an avenue to vent thoughts and emotions which otherwise overwhelmed me. For over seven years, I sought the right to what I believed was innately mine—motherhood. And during those years, I wrote my way through each pain point as I forged my way to overcome biological instinct and find the resolve to accept what is.

Perhaps it is the habit of comparing myself to people with greater challenges than me that I deem myself to be fine and ordinary. I appreciate that we all process experiences differently. A situation which poses a significant challenge to one person may not have much of an impact on another. Degrees of challenge, therefore, cannot be directly compared. All the same, my recent exposure to the depth of sadness, anguish, and pain of people all around me made me wonder whether my story would, in fact, be worth telling.

The other night, I came across an illustration of intersex genitals (thanks to "The Vulva Gallery" on Instagram). It wasn't the picture so much as the accompanying story which tugged my attention.

> "Because I was born in this form, a hundred photos have been taken, a thousand hands have touched, a million eyes have looked, none with my consent. All of the doctors, they call me unwanted. In a world that says I am broken, undesirable, and need to be 'fixed', this image is mine to share. To the eyes I want to see. Behold the power; the beauty. My intersex vulva. My perfection."

As I read this, I sighed with a heaviness around the unappreciated ease of my life, purely because of *my* form. I tried to imagine what it must have been like for her to grow up in her body before she found a love for her own perfection. I thought about her parents and imagined their thoughts and feelings the moment she was born, immediately foreseeing the potential challenges ahead in their child's life. Later, over dinner, my husband wasn't ready for me to talk this through in all of the detail with which I wanted to delve. Fair. I shelved the thoughts which continued to spin silently and heavily as we engaged in other topics.

The next morning, I woke to some family news which dropped me back into sadness, this time for my eleven-year-old nephew. I thought about his illness, his symptoms, his reality, his struggles, his pain—on many levels. The need to help him consumed my thoughts, spinning around the question, *how . . . how?*

I abruptly collected myself as I had a client consultation at ten o'clock that morning. It was with a yogi from one of my Yin classes who was drawn to the emotional intelligence part of my teachings. She downloaded her story in detail and shared the sadness she experienced in her day-to-day world. Before that call, she was just a beautiful soul in my yoga class. I knew she was getting a lot out of the classes from the hugs and tears she shared with me following each class. Now, though, I recognise her as someone who uses yoga as her clutch to sanity, freedom, independence and to reclaim herself outside of her home environment.

The afternoon brought another consultation with a student from a different yoga class. Again, before that consultation, she was just a student on the mat who was there for her own reasons. She always showed up 100% to each practice. I could see she wanted and needed every class she attended. In our consult, she shared her past with me and explained her present situation. We strategically worked through her story until we found new perspectives which led to relief, gratitude and love for those experiences and her life path.

The evening came and I fronted up at the studio to teach my Tuesday night class. One guy came in who had been to my classes before. He has a round, kind face, soft voice, and a gentle demeanour, though he didn't smile when he greeted me. The first time he came to my class, I asked the standard question about "injuries or anything else going on that I need to know about". He told me that he was sick, a problem with his heart. He must be in his mid-thirties. His expression was not one of sadness or desperation. It was empty. It was a look of resignation. I welcomed him back into class and, during the long-held poses, I lay my hands on him to ease him in. He felt lonely—the loneliness of someone who knows that ultimately no one else is in this with him, regardless of how many people love him and cling to him on the sidelines.

To his left, there was a sweet girl in her twenties who breathes heavily and contorts her face as soon she closes her eyes during each pose. She's a regular of mine and I have come to find that this muscular twisting and convulsing is a normal part of her reality. I don't know what's going on for her, but appreciate that there is likely a deep story behind the front she allows the public to see.

On the other side of her was a man, maybe forty, who periodically moaned throughout the class. I sought permission to rest my hands on his back to reassure him that, in that moment, he was safe.

At the back of the studio, was a lady who was very underweight. She was comfortable with my hands-on approach throughout class; however, as I touched my hands to her head in Savasana (the resting pose which closes each class), she quickly, yet very politely, declined my touch. I realised that she was wearing a wig.

The reason I started practising yoga initially was to balance out my fast-paced, coffee-fuelled, frantic corporate high. What began as a mental practice turned into a physical practice as my head cooled and my body started taking on the benefits of yoga. Now, here I was, guiding people through yoga for reasons of their own, and gaining an appreciation for just how debilitating some of their issues were. These students weren't simply stressed from work.

I look across the table at my friend sipping her coffee. She nods at me to continue, giving me the space for my thoughts and insecurities to be heard.

> "My life has been one of a consistent comfort level; my highs and lows never straying far from *fine*. Knowing this ironically gives me some sort of uneasiness ... what is this that I'm feeling? Is it a level of bashfulness for coasting through life while those around me experience real and genuine pain? Is it a sense of naivety around flying the flag of 'I can help you' when, in reality, I have never experienced the turmoil and deep pain that some people feel? All the while, I cannot withhold my skills nor deny

my passion to help. It's not as if I should only work with people who mirror my exact life experiences. That doesn't make any sense. And I have more to offer than that."

I zig zag back and forth in my thinking, pouring it all out on the table. I question the strength of my qualifications, weighing up how theory and practice meet with personal life experiences. I question all of this despite having witnessed the genuinely liberating and long-lasting changes that occur in my clients during our consultations. Their testimonials speak volumes. The results are profound and continue to inspire the bejesus out of me, coaxing me to continue to reach more and more people in this way.

And maybe I have touched trauma in my own way. I have felt desperation for life. I touched my version of dying a slow death. If trauma, by definition, is a distressing event over which we feel we have no control, my experience qualifies. I faced this challenge head on, and I worked through it—each time, each facet, again and again. I continue to apply the work as new emotions and upsetting thoughts arise. I am not afraid of feeling the big, heavy, supposedly negative emotions anymore, because I trust that I have the capacity to work through them. Could this be what helps to stabilise me and keep me on solid ground so I may guide people out of their depths? The trust I have in my own capacity allows me to believe that others have this same capacity. I am merely here to facilitate their experience in finding it.

I finish unpacking all of this baggage right back at

my friend.

"I'm fine. And I'm working through it."

Big, heartfelt grins are exchanged across the table in recognition of our long overdue catch up.

The Art of Conversation

Two weeks ago, I turned forty-two. I don't *think* I have any preconceived notions about the forties as a significant turning point, the start of 'the downhill slide', as some refer to it. My age now is simply one year after forty-one, which is the year after forty. They're all essentially the same to me. Yet, this year, things physically changed—almost on cue. The knuckle on the middle finger of my right hand feels as if I've bashed it and the whole joint aches and feels stiff. My husband suggests it might be the start of arthritis.

"Hmmm . . . maybe."

Best to outwardly acknowledge, but inwardly dismiss suggestions like that. I don't do arthritis, especially not this early. I'm not interested in staring down the barrel of carrying it for forty-plus years into the future. Thanks anyway.

I visit my parents up on the north coast and stay there for a few days for some quality catch up time. While I'm rubbing comfrey ointment into my finger one night, I explain the feeling to my mum.

"Sounds like arthritis."

Pfffff . . . you people are in cahoots. I need to chat with my middle finger directly rather than being spooked by these other suggestions.

I have a history of having meaningful conversations with my body parts. It started in 2008 when I broke up with my then boyfriend. Although I knew it was for the best and felt a great sense of relief, I still held the weight of sadness and grief for an imagined future which was no longer to be. I lay in bed one night with a knot in my stomach, literally. I rested my hands on the area which felt similar to a cramp, yet slightly raised, sticking out of my belly like a misplaced organ. I started a throw-away conversation with it as I was drifting off to sleep.

What is this feeling? What are you trying to tell me? Immediately, everything cleared in my field of vision, and it was just me and, in front of me, a little boy. He was crying, bawling actually. This was not a child who was putting it on for attention or to get his own way. He was genuinely heartbroken, devastated. I tried to console him, just being there with him. I asked him what was wrong, and he told me he had been waiting, and that soon he was going to come to me to be my son, but now, because I had ended my relationship, he wouldn't be coming. The tears were those of someone who had just been denied life—by his own mother. I sat down next to him and explained that the man he saw me with wasn't really his dad, that was just the man who I was with at the time. I reassured him that his dad was someone else, somewhere else.

> "Tell you what, it's going to be easier for you to find your dad, from the space where you are, rather than me finding him from here. So why don't you go and find him and tell him where I am?"

The little boy's tears dried, his faced brightened, and the very moment he agreed and turned to run off and find his dad, I was snapped back into reality by an abrupt shift in my belly as the bulge under my hands dropped away. It woke me and startled me at the same time. I stared at the ceiling for a few moments, taking stock of what had just happened. My hands were still resting on my belly, but now they were simply laying on top of skin and the everyday digestion processes going on somewhere beneath them.

That was in June. I met Joel in October. Whether it was my little boy who found him and excitedly dragged him by the hand to my door, or the weekend course I attended which allowed me to tap into something greater, I don't mind. Perhaps it was both coming into alignment. I never met my little boy, though. Sometimes I wonder if, one day, I'll meet this soul somewhere along the road, and we'll recognise each other without knowing why. We'll feel an inner knowing and the recognition of a deep, untold connection, but without any conscious awareness of what it means or where it came from.

That conversation with the little boy was in 2008. Fast forward to 2018 when I attended my first yoga training, and part of term three was spent at an ashram. Whilst there, we observed noble silence each morning upon waking, maintaining it throughout our yoga practice, into our meditation and continuing until after breakfast. By the third day, I was enjoying sinking into silence and appreciating the lack of small talk within the group.

In one of the morning meditations, it was suggested that we settle our awareness on what is referred to in yogic philosophy as a *chakra* (an energy centre in the body). I slowly slid my focus up and down my spine, scanning for any area that felt sticky, asking for my attention. My upper abdomen, otherwise known as the solar plexus area, felt appealing. I stayed with the feeling, resting my attention there without expecting anything in particular. Then a conversation sparked up organically. We shared a bit of back-and-forth banter, and my solar plexus was seemingly answering back of its own accord, playing a co-lead role in our dialogue without my conscious input. It turns out my solar plexus has quite the sense of humour—sarcastic, in fact! But I couldn't laugh. *Noble silence.* I suddenly felt like a ten-year-old at school who was playing up with a friend and trying not to get caught by the teacher. I was trying so hard not to laugh out loud, but the harder I tried, the funnier my solar plexus became and the more jokes it cracked—at my expense. At one point, I started to fidget, adjusting my posture to make it more upright and face the front, as if that would subdue my distraction and help me restrain the belly laughter which was now threatening to expose both of us. The voice from within piped up with a sarcastic,

"Genius. *That* will help . . ."

It didn't let up.

Whenever you're trying hard not to laugh, there's something about that scene that makes everything funnier. The craziness continued and grew until I yanked my pashmina all the way over my head to hide the teeth-baring grin on my face, eyes still closed. Under the yellow tinge of my pashmina, my solar plexus and I silently giggled together. It was a bonding moment.

Then came 2019. I woke up feeling a bit 'germy'. That feeling of a flu coming on—achy shoulders, achy back. For me, these symptoms are normally the precursor to the flu. In recent years, I'd become more curious, each time I was sick, about whether there was a psychosomatic component. I was curious about the underlying benefits potentially gained from having those symptoms. With that line of questioning, I became aware that each time I was taken down by the flu, what I was really craving during that period was downtime, thinking time, rest time—essentially just *time*. After a few years of observation and chalking up results, it became apparent to me that when I didn't intentionally stop and make time for myself, I would generally bring on a virus. My body steps in with an *I've got this* flag. I'm forced to the couch, and suddenly I have time for me.

This time was different though. I didn't feel rushed

or stressed about anything. I didn't feel my time was being compromised at all, and I was strategically doing everything I wanted to do. These viral symptoms, therefore, came without the standard explanation.

I pulled out my bolster to sit down and meditate. First, a few breaths to settle. In my mind's eye, I stepped into a white room with cushions and beanbags. There was soft, warm light in the room, perfect for an unintimidating round table discussion, so to speak. Into the room, I invited the virus, as well as my immune system. We acquainted ourselves and I opened up a discussion between the three of us:

"Okay. What's going on here?"

The virus started laughing and said it had no idea, finding the whole scene comical that it's circulating through my body without understanding why. I turned to my immune system, which looked sheepish, even embarrassed.

"I was busy doing other things. I guess I just moved my focus elsewhere."

I asked where its focus had moved to. Awkward silence. I laid my hands on different parts of my body and asked, "Here?" I kept moving them around with each "Nope, not there", until I received a few yesses. The yesses were related to freckles and moles on my skin that I'd been meaning to get checked by a specialist. It had been on my mental to-do list and I would frequently think of it at random times, but then forget about, so I hadn't made the doctor's appointment as intended. The worry about them was obviously sitting within—and apparently my immune system took up the call.

So, I ask, "Are you focusing on these areas because it's required, or because of my worry?"

"Your worry."

We proceed to have a conversation, clarifying that the immune system has my complete permission to attend to what is tangible, rather than getting distracted by what's in my thoughts. I also promised that I would make an appointment with the skin specialist immediately, to remove the worry lingering within my subconscious.

I personally thanked my immune system for taking one for the team and totally stepping up to protect me. My immune system felt appreciated, and we gave each other one of those long-sustained, heart-to-heart hugs. We invited the virus in for a group hug as well; after all, it was the virus who allowed this conversation and gave me what felt like a profound recognition that my immune system is truly on my side, doing as I ask. The virus suddenly had a purpose, and, with that, it vanished out of the hug, leaving the two of us behind.

My immune system asked for four hours to get everything back to normal again. Deal.

Once out of the meditation, I made my doctor's appointment for a skin check. Locked in. Later that day, no germy feeling. No flu.

Given the previous conversations I'd had with various body parts, none of this seemed weird at the time. In fact, it seemed perfectly normal and quite logical. It felt like a genuine conversation and beautiful way to connect with my physical being. I appreciate that there is a time for medication and there is a time for meditation. What I determined through this experience, was that meditation can be a perfect first port of call.

A little while after this, a modality called craniosacral therapy came into my periphery. I didn't know much about it, but I wondered whether it would be appropriate for my eleven-year-old nephew who was sick. I thought I should try the therapy myself first to decide whether I could recommend it. In twenty minutes of questioning about my history and health, the therapist homed in on my years of unsuccessful attempts to fall pregnant, despite me assuring her that I had made peace with my reality. She was pushing to trigger a pain spot, but I was quite grounded in my resolve. I felt comfortable with the outcome, grateful in fact.

I lay down on the table, took several deep breaths and relaxed into the moment. She placed her hands on my body and asked me to notice whatever arose, whether that be physical sensations, emotions or thoughts. When she put her hands on each side of my hips, the whole area started to overheat, as if under a heat lamp. She suggested that my right ovary was sad about losing the opportunity to bear children. Without continuing that conversation with the therapist, I went straight in and sat with my right ovary. It was like sitting down over a cup of tea where there was no need for small talk. Silence was welcomed. We could chat, but only if there was something worthwhile to say.

My right ovary *was* sad. I let it talk and I heard it out. The grief. The loss. The redundancy and lack of purpose. Then I offered it a deal.

> "What if, every time I lay my hands on somebody, whether it's a hug or adjusting somebody in a yoga posture, the essence of this touch comes directly from you. The nurturing that comes through that touch is a mothering touch that is all you, where you are able to nurture hundreds, even thousands of people."

My right ovary agreed it was a good idea and relaxed with a renewed sense of purpose.

Sometimes I wonder what might have eventuated if I hadn't had this chat with my ovary. I'll never know whether the sadness within this part of my body would have stayed there and become something more sinister. I'm happy not to know. What I do know is that I continue to receive many comments at the end of my yoga classes about my "magic hands", or that my touch transports people, or that they could feel an electric buzz throughout their body while my hands were on them. All of these comments are received by me without taking any personal credit; rather I check in with my right ovary to make sure that it heard the feedback and gratitude from people who felt mothered as a result.

So, I'm ready to chat with my middle finger about this so-called arthritis. In this situation though, it feels that I would benefit from seeing a doctor first to gain any official medical insights, which I can then ask my finger about directly.

The Finger & The Party

I get along to the doctor and I wave my stiff and swollen finger at him, wondering what he has to say about it. Not much, it turns out.

"Rub some anti-inflammatory cream on it and see what happens."

Wow. Thanks.

I head straight home, pull out the boswellia and devil's claw tablets from my medicine cabinet, and commit to buying curcumin the next time I'm at the shops. I continue to rub comfrey ointment on my fingers and knuckles. In the absence of any medical intervention, I feel content with applying my own anti-inflammatory protocol.

Out comes my meditation bolster and onto the

sheepskin rug. I sit myself down and prepare for a chat with my finger. First, I feel my breath—it flows easily and slowly, unconfined, like an old romantic movie that you could watch for hours on a rainy day. Following the rhythm of my breath becomes meditative, and I feel myself settle into a kind of stupor. The world outside ceases to hold my attention.

I have a ritual with which I often start my meditations. First, I imagine myself connecting with the earth; the material, tangible part of me that needs to understand things in a practical way. Once I feel that connection streaming from the core of the earth into my body, I draw the feeling right up into my heart and imagine it settling there. Then another search happens above me. With my imagination, I reach far off into the cosmos, connecting with the non-tangible part of me, the soul, the energy of life, the universal consciousness. I often feel as if I'm tapping into collective or cosmic consciousness of the all-knowing, all-seeing, and all-loving. Whilst there, I request to tap into the divine vision of this whole experience, recognising it to be perfect, exactly as it is. I draw this awareness down, into my heart. We may be spiritual beings having a physical experience or physical beings having a spiritual experience. I find both to be true, and I call both truths into my heart where they intertwine as one truth.

And then I feel ready.

"Hello middle finger. What's up?"

Not overly talkative, but I am told, loud and clear,

that I need to pull back from *doing, doing* all the time. I was quietly hoping for something more profound than that, but I'm happy to take the message at face value, apply it as much as I can talk myself into, then see what happens.

The conversation was shorter than anticipated. I'm not ready to end my meditation just yet. So, while I'm here, about that feeling of defeat . . .

I regularly facilitate a four-week Yoga Nidra guided meditation program for a small group of about fifteen people. I work with the 'Integrative Restoration' style of Yoga Nidra, which is a relatively new technique combining the more traditional Yoga Nidra with Western psychology and modern neuroscience. The magical aspect of this practice, in a practical sense, is that it allows us to bring a specific emotion to mind and simply hold it, feel it. We stay with the emotion and become aware of the physical aspects of it—becoming familiar with how the body experiences this emotion. Before beginning each new program, I invite each of the attendees to let me know which emotions they currently feel burdened by. The accompanying story doesn't need to be explained, just the emotions they are feeling because of their story. The purpose is for me to address every one of their nominated emotions over the course. That way, each person will have an alternate method of potentially moving through their emotions.

As part of the upcoming program, the emotion put forward by one of the attendees is *defeat*. Everything I teach to others I like to experience myself first. Of course,

I appreciate that my experience is unique to me; all the same, I at least have my own experience to draw on. So, to prepare myself for leading the 'defeat' meditation, yesterday I settled down onto my bolster to feel defeat.

When I noticed how defeat was showing up as a physical sensation in my body, I watched a shape that resembled a deflated balloon slide in slow motion down the interior of my body. Like algae, it slowly slimed all the way down, bottoming out in my empty womb. And then it just lay there, like a lifeless blob. That certainly was Defeat, personified. It just lay there, so I just sat there, staring at it, wondering what my appropriate reaction should be. My reflex was to cheer it up; like buying a drink for someone you find slumped in a chair in the corner of a pumping party. The absolute lack of response was very clear feedback that this was not the right approach. I ended up just sitting there, being with it. The party continued and I watched from the outskirts while Defeat looked downward, oblivious to the music.

I felt unprepared for meeting Defeat, perhaps unskilled. I hoped that simply being there together was enough in that moment. I didn't know what else to do. I stayed for a while and then, when it felt appropriate to leave, asked Defeat if I could come back another time.

So, today, after my middle finger gave me briefer-than-expected company, I decide to knock on Defeat's door once again to ask if I could join it. We sit again. Nothing is forthcoming from the other side; this is all going to be on me.

This time, as I sit here, bottomed out in this empty

womb with Defeat, I realise that my intention to fix Defeat was completely misplaced. Defeat is exactly that, *the feeling of defeat*. I was previously trying to convert it into something else and thereby requesting it to dissolve out of existence. How fucking rude of me! I was asking this emotion to be what it wasn't. The emotion is already defeated, literally, and now I am essentially calling it useless, unnecessary, and redundant? Ouch . . . back up.

We sit together, and this time I appreciate Defeat for being what it is. And so, I just stay, allowing it to be that way. Remembering the step from practicing Yoga Nidra myself, I now welcome Defeat in, exactly as it is, as part of my human experience. This emotion is a part of who I am. We become friends, accepting each other exactly the way we are, and I instantly feel more whole.

Symptoms Are Just the Messengers

With my finger revving up other forty-two-year-old aches and pains in my body, I notice that my back is starting to twinge a lot. I spend all of November teaching like a Trojan, covering other teachers' yoga classes while they are holidaying or sick, on top of my regular schedule. November is busy, but I know that everything will quieten down in December—and December is just around the corner. *Hang in there.*

The last weekend in November is a dramatic climax with respect to the number of classes I teach. I stupidly try to push through it. It turns out that my body can't hang in there. I come undone. The pain in my back is now extreme. I literally couldn't teach another class if I tried. I can't move properly. I can stand and I can sit (but not for too long) and that's about the end of it. When signing up to Yoga Teacher Training, I had hoped that one of the inclusions was eternal immunity to injury, but I'm finding out now that this was not the case.

I am wishing I had taken my finger's advice to stop *doing, doing.*

My back pain takes me out of action for two weeks and my drug-free body suddenly finds me eating anti-inflammatories and pain relief tablets for breakfast. There's an inner voice throwing stones from behind a barricade, with a placard that says, 'Practice what you preach', referring to finding balance in life.

Then my left ovary starts to swell and become tender. It turns out there are twenty-three cysts on it, one especially large; yet none of them pose a problem, as far as the Western doctor I consult is concerned. Once I have this reassurance from the doctor, I head straight to my acupuncturist. Within days, both the ovary and my back have begun to settle. I'm not completely better, but at least okay enough to gingerly carry my backpack on and off the plane. Tomorrow, I fly to Bali to attend another yoga training. It's my turn to be a student again.

Despite my awkward manoeuvres to shove my carry-on luggage into the overhead locker, and the just-as-awkward retrieval as we land in Denpasar, my back holds up. It also passes the car test after our driver seemingly chooses the bumpiest road he can find to take us to Ubud. Now that I've made it here, unbroken, I have a few days to enjoy some gentle walks around town before training starts.

My travelling companion and I eat at some delicious cafés and maintain a somewhat boring standard of only eating at 'safe' eateries. Despite these efforts, on day three, 'Bali Belly' sets in. I dart off the main street and up a conveniently located laneway behind a line of shops and restaurants, where some of the staff are on their cigarette break. Crouching down to the ground, stabilising myself against a wall with one hand while holding back my hair with the other, I heave up my breakfast onto a pile of dirt and rubble right in front of the smokers. After wiping away a little bit of spew and dribble from my mouth, I hesitantly lift my gaze so I can attempt some sort of etiquette and apologise to my spectators.

Then comes the weird walk you do when you're trying to get somewhere quickly, yet, at the same time, move your body very slowly. I do this weird walk all the way back to my homestay where I continue to 'cleanse'. My saving grace is that all this vomiting doesn't re-injure my back—not that this occurs to me at the time. The only thought I have in the moment is *must not leave bathroom*.

After a solid night's sleep, I feel mostly stable, albeit completely drained of energy. I don't get out of bed. Day turns to night and I continue to sleep, sweat, sleep, sweat through the night. In the morning, after a cold shower, I am able to perk myself up like a committed student, ready for the first day of training.

Within a couple of days, I notice my bodily functions changing with additional symptoms that I immediately recognise as parasites, after being diagnosed with parasites from my Cambodian iced tea drinking episode. I am all too familiar with parasite protocol and start it immediately. There goes all of my food joy. No more sugars of any description. No fruit. No young coconuts. No coconut ice cream that I had vowed to eat daily. No sweet vegetables. Limited carbohydrates. Raw garlic at breakfast and dinner. Pumpkin seeds and sunflower seeds for lunch. Anti-parasite herbal tablets. After a few days on this diet, I fast for twenty-four hours, water only. Then back onto the loveless diet promoting parasite starvation and demise.

By the end of the ten-day training, I am starting to stabilise and feel better. We have one free day before my girlfriend and I fly home in the evening, so I take the opportunity to catch up with another friend of mine who lives in Ubud. He and I visit his new soon-to-be-finished house, and then the Green School campus (an international school set up on a model of sustainability) where his daughter is doing her final year of high school. We go to the Pyramids of Chi for an afternoon drink and to catch up on all things . . . until . . .

I very quickly excuse myself and only just make it inside the restroom door before my stomach up-ends itself. Given that I only make it as far as the sink, not the toilet cubicle, I spend a few minutes removing the largest chunks of food with paper towel, and then push the remaining smaller bits of regurgitated carrot and spinach down the drain, praying nobody walks in. When I eventually resurface, my friend puts me on the back of his scooter to return me to my homestay. We make an unscheduled stop en route so I can expel the remaining contents of my stomach onto the side of the street. I don't recall ever spewing in public whilst being sober, yet here I am on this trip becoming quite familiar with this activity.

Back at the homestay, my hosts show me to the communal bathroom downstairs, having already checked me out of my room. I lie on the cold-tiled floor at the base of the toilet. Any further away from the toilet is pure risk taking—and potentially messy. My girlfriend comes to see me, takes a few obligatory photos of me in this pitiful state, then reassures me that I am fine and that I *am* getting on that plane tonight.

> "I'm arranging a bucket for you for the car. I don't mind how you use it, nor which end it comes out of, but we're going to the airport."

Thankfully, I only use the bucket once, and it's for contents which exit the more appropriate end when you're sharing a car with two other people.

I sleep on the flight home. My husband picks me up at Sydney airport, and as soon as I feel his arms around me, I emotionally collapse. I am spent; absolutely depleted.

A good night's sleep does me wonders and, over the next two days, I start to feel almost normal again, until that germy feeling starts in the muscles, that feeling like the flu is coming. That's when I crack it. *WTF*. I am rarely sick, and yet, I have had an assortment of continuous overlapping ailments for two months and am now to the point of getting angry about it. A client cum friend kindly reflects my own line of questioning back at me:

"What is all of this about? There's some underlying link why all of this going on. So, Sherrie, what is it?"

Worthy question. I have been feeling so shitty about the whole rolling-ailments experience that I haven't held my head high enough to see the question I need to ask myself most. What *is* this about?

Back to my meditation seat. *What am I getting out of this experience? What are the benefits to having all these ailments? Is it for the attention?* Something twinges within. *Attention from me? Focusing on myself? Or attention from other people?* Another twinge. Oooh ... getting warmer ... *Care?* A shift within. Bingo! Yes, I want to feel cared for.

As soon as I find these words, I feel them directly touch a raw nerve inside and I am certain that's the reason for my assortment of ailments. Over the past year and a half, I had been feeling increasingly uncared for by certain people in my circles. It may have been a comment here and there, and those comments may well have been surrounded by other words of utter care, but something in my attention clutched onto the non-caring actions and words, and subconsciously accumulated them all to the point where they created a soap box for me to stand on to demand care be given.

Back pain, when you can't move and are completely in somebody else's care, will definitely tick that box.

Twenty-three cysts will also garner a dose of required attention—'specialist' attention, at that.

Being debilitatingly sick in another country and feeling so vulnerable, not even being able to leave my room for a fundamental ingredient like drinking water, definitely called for extra and personalised care from my host—who was amazing, checking in on me and making sure I had what I needed.

I was doing it. I was creating situations where I *needed* care, purely to make it obvious to my conscious mind that I am, in fact, cared for. It was a call for attention. Or rather, it was a call to *redirect my attention* and refocus my perspective to notice that I was, in fact, already being cared for. I now need to recognise that my wayward narrow focus was on all the places where I wasn't feeling cared for, noticing experiences on only one end of the spectrum.

I start noticing where care *is* apparent in my life. Throughout all of these experiences, my husband has given me unwavering and constant care. As have my parents.

Now that I can properly address the perception of lack and, instead, refocus my attention to where it *is* being fulfilled and how it isn't missing at all, I can let the symptoms settle back down. And they do. They really are just the messengers—very effective ones at that. They collectively served their purpose to highlight my imbalanced perceptions, allowing me to wrap my conscious awareness around the thoughts and emotions that were piling up subconsciously.

To me, this is a healthy working system; one that communicates with its owner, calling attention to what is otherwise being overlooked. The more challenging aspect is our role in that dialogue. It depends on our willingness to openly listen to our symptoms *as messengers*, and then work with whatever comes up in that space. It's also having people in our life who will pose the right questions when you are otherwise swamped in self-pity and vomit.

And now that I have heard the message, loud and clear, and consciously found all the places where I am thoroughly cared for, it's time to create a self-care plan for ongoing recognition of care—doubling as a strategy to avoid revisiting the road of multiple ailments.

Connecting Dots

I book an appointment to see my acupuncturist solely for maintenance and well-being. I book a chiropractor appointment. I revisit my diet, noting that it has slowly transitioned back to being highly acidic. I buy a tonne of kale and it goes into almost everything I eat, starting with my chocolate breakfast smoothie, made of kale, carrot, beetroot, cucumber, banana, cinnamon, cacao, and a bunch of supplements for good measure. My own tried and tested self-care protocol is in full swing. I maintain my daily meditation and yoga practice, no matter what time it is and what else I have going on that day. I arrange a few catch ups with girlfriends, creating opportunities to be hugged and heard. I reunite with friends who I adore, but find that our misaligning schedules ordinarily keep us apart. Right now, I'm all about reconnecting with the special people in my life who nurse my heart and pour out reciprocated care.

All these self-care practices turn out to be strategically in place just in time to learn that my brother, Shane, has found a lump in his neck. The doctor immediately refers to it as a tumour, without any appreciation for the frightening connotations of this word. We stand by while Shane goes through the motions of visiting specialists and having biopsies, until the answer comes back that the tumour is malignant. He and I both remain very pragmatic (at face value) as we move through a conversation about the next steps. I even manage to quote a one-liner from the movie, *Ferris Bueller's Day Off*, where Ferris says to Cameron: "You're not dying, you just can't think of anything better to do".

I call my parents to make sure they're okay after hearing the news. I call my cousin Brett and bring him up to speed. Right now, his support is what I need. After we cover everybody else, Brett asks how I'm doing.

> "I feel mostly stable, just a little shaken, but calm. It's huge news, but it's one step at a time, right?"

I call my parents back, double checking that they're *actually* okay. I call my brother again.

I need yoga. Now.

I arrive early so I can sit in solitude for thirty minutes before class. The studio is only five minutes from my home, but five minutes is long enough for an anxious imagination to run too far in the wrong direction. I need to contain it.

I kneel onto my mat, eyes closed, soft music in the background. My mind is fighting to stay in the present moment. The teacher, who is also a friend of mine, disarms me with what should be a relatively harmless question.

"How are you, Sherrie?"

"I'm a little fragile."

And then the tears come.

We wait to get more information and a date for Shane's surgery. Once the cancerous lump is removed and examined, they'll then be able to determine the next course of action.

As I sit here, I mentally connect the dots. I realise the benefit of my recent journey; learning what it is that I need to do, see and hear, in order to feel cared for. I am now comprehending the bigger picture and the importance of putting all of those practices, appointments and catch-ups in place to prepare me for what is ahead. I am overwhelmingly appreciative of the value of that entire experience. I get the feeling that was a necessary lesson for me to prepare for this upcoming period of emotional and mental care for my brother. All my attention now turns toward him.

On the morning of the surgery, I pick up Shane early to allow for Sydney traffic at that time of day. It turns out we are early enough to beat the anticipated rush hour, and we arrive at the hospital with plenty of time to spare. There's a stiff, brand-new-looking blue and green couch in the hospital lobby. That will do. Somewhere to wait. The ceiling is about ten stories above us, not nearly close enough to keep a lid on my anxious thoughts. I buy myself a takeaway coffee and toast, which Shane watches me eat, unable to eat anything himself pre-operation. Small talk is key. It's all I can manage under the pressure of my racing heartbeat. Shane's humour, on the other hand, is surprisingly maintained with jokes rolling off his tongue naturally.

We step into the elevator to go up to level three. Before the doors close, two people step in with us who look like they are further down the road on their cancer journey. They are pale and gaunt, wearing hats and crocheted beanies to cover their balding heads. The confronting nature of this reality cuts deep, giving us insight into what potentially awaits. Shane seems remarkably calm. I hold it together—just. It isn't until I leave him so he can get changed into his hospital gown that I lose it and, as much as I try, cannot regain composure. I walk back into his ward and he stops listening to the nurse's pre-op instructions and gives me that big brother *I know you, you can't lie to me* look as I try to act as if I am there to support him, not the other way around. After ten minutes of my feeble attempt, and zero success stopping the tears, he sends me home.

I cry the whole way.

While my big brother is in surgery, I am recognising my inability to be still, combined with the great need to be still. I have to slow my racing mind. My action-packed imagination is darting off on long tangents with dark detailed scenarios and conversations that haven't even happened—and may never happen. I need meditation to bring me back. It locks my mind in the present moment of my *actual* reality, not my imagination. If I can attach to this and this only, I can still my mind. And so, I head outside to take a walk and get some fresh air.

I grab the opportunity for an open-eyed meditation with the intention of tethering my focus to the present moment. I need to reign in the worrying part of me. As I'm walking, I silently label everything my attention lands on from moment to moment. My walk has a narrative along the lines of: *long grass . . . wet sand . . . man with shopping bag . . . dog . . . crack in pavement . . . cloud . . . fallen leaves . . . white car . . . bad window tint . . . step right foot . . . left foot . . . right foot . . . left foot . . . puddle . . .* I just need to be *here right now*, and that is all.

Arriving back home, with my nervous system somewhat calmer, I can now consider sitting down to a Yoga Nidra meditation. I take a few moments to properly identify the specific emotion which is most pressing so I may just sit with it, feeling into it. It's despair; I feel a sense of hopelessness.

I sit. I close my eyes. I breathe—deeply, slowly and deliberately. I allow myself to feel Despair. I stay with this feeling until I own it, welcoming in this emotion as part of my present experience. As I begin to investigate how this emotion is experienced in my body as physical sensation, it feels as if my legs turn to jelly and my sense of stable ground falls away. I acknowledge all of this as Despair and simply allow it to be this way. Then I bring to mind the opposite emotion to Despair, which, in this context, is Hope and Positivity. When I feel these emotions and notice their physical attributes in my body, I feel a buoyant sense of strength arise in my upper body, specifically around my chest and arms. And so, as per the process of Yoga Nidra, I move back and forth between the two, feeling each of these emotions one at a time, before pulling these opposing feelings into my awareness to experience them simultaneously. As I do this, my legs remain like jelly, dormant beneath me. Yet, I have a vivid sense that even if I can no longer stand, given these legs of jelly, and am lying on the floor in despair, I have the upper body strength to drag myself through this by my forearms. Even if it is a struggle to pull myself through this next phase of life, here in this moment, I recognise that I *do* have the strength to move *through* it, no matter what that may look like.

I stay in my meditation seat for I don't know how long, just breathing full, deep breaths.

With my fears remaining and a sustained sense of despair still present, at least they are now in check. These emotions can remain, acknowledged and felt, while I simultaneously acknowledge my ability to access an over-arching strength to do what I need to do to be there for my brother.

I leave my bolster to go and find Joel. We sit down on our lounge, talking it all through as it happens—including all the 'what ifs' regarding the outcome of Shane's surgery. I can articulate all of my emotions about Shane. He is my primary concern. There is a secondary concern though, which has mostly been suppressed, remaining silent from the outside world. It is my concern for me and my future, specifically relating to my marriage. If Shane should exit life in this process, his kids will remain with their mum as a single parent. And if something should ever happen to her, I would assume responsibility for those four kids without a second thought. Knowing this, an underlying fear creeps in around what that would mean for Joel's and my future as a couple. We have finally carved out a child-free future which inspires both of us. How would it be for Joel to abandon the future we've visioned together to take on four kids that aren't his own? Four! What scares me is my deep-seated priority to my nephews and nieces, and whether Joel would feel backed into a corner if I were to step forward to fill that role as their guardian. Without saying any of these thoughts out loud to Joel, he just holds me. After a little while, he breaks the silence, suggesting that one of the scariest things is not knowing what will happen. He slowly and gently talks through each potential outcome, as if bringing it to the surface will forge some level of peace with whatever may come. Then it's as if he reads my mind.

> "If this doesn't work out well for Shane, and Sharon needs our support for the kids, then we'll do whatever we need to. If something

happens to Sharon, and we need to sell our apartment and move to the suburbs to buy a house, and raise those four kids, then that's what we'll do."

I don't know if it's possible for a heart to break under the weight of overwhelming love for one human, but that's what it feels like. My heart explodes internally. My eyes well with tears of relief. I am filled with love and gratitude for this incredible human I married, and with fear, with anxiety and with peace. I feel it all present in this moment.

I quietly wonder whether the solidarity of our marriage is the source of the upper body strength that I felt in my meditation, this capacity to pull myself through whatever may come. Likely. All I know is that my heart is full. I appreciate that this is life. This is how it goes, always moving, up and down, experiences unravelling. Life unfolding.

Feeling ready for the next step in this journey, I head back to hospital, walk into the great lobby, pass the uncomfortable blue and green couch, and take the elevator to the recovery ward.

Shane smiles at me. While he opens a cooler bag with a pre-made salad from home, he describes the crap food offered in hospital and offers to share his lunch with me.

It is a long two-week wait before the doctor delivers

the results to Shane that this was a rather aggressive cancer which had wormed itself into Shane's lymph node. Fortunately, the cancer had remained encapsulated, and so the surgeon was confident that he'd removed it completely. He was laughing at Shane's easy attitude around the whole situation, noting that he had just had a life-threatening situation, and yet here he was walking into the surgeon's office for his results like a rock star. That's Shane.

We never know what is around the corner. It could be an illness, a cyclone or some other misfortune coming our way, we don't know. But for now, I feel like I have my brother back to stay. I exhale and return to my version of normal.

Queen Bee

It has taken me a few days to readjust my focus onto my path. I'm back now and feel like my thinking has returned to normality where I have full access to my thoughts. I can teach a yoga class with presence once again.

One class is business as usual. People laying on their mats, moving in and out of Yin yoga poses and then rolling into Savasana at the end of class. During Savasana, a girl at the front of the studio starts to shake. Her whole upper body quivers from side to side. I've had people faint and have seizures in previous classes, so I feel somewhat prepared, while hoping that she'll stop shaking and we can avoid a potential emergency. I reach over and lightly touch her ankle as a kind of *you're safe* gesture. Her body settles and we both calm. I've seen her just once before. She came to my class last week, but I have no idea of her background or medical history and whether this is something that I need to be aware of for future classes.

When class ends, I ask her if she knew that she was shaking during Savasana.

"Sometimes that happens."

"Are you unwell?"

"No. I have visions and sometimes, when I do, that happens. You were in this vision, and it made me sad. I started crying. You were wearing blue and you were surrounded by people, like you were on a mountain top. And there were nappies everywhere. There was blue everywhere, dark, royal blue. Blue nappies. And there were bees, lots of bees, but it seemed that you were the queen bee. It was sad, like something was missing. But it was happy too. You need to go to a kingdom, like Mongolia or something."

Random. I don't know how I feel about this girl's vision. The vision I hold for myself *is* to mother many, a kind of queen bee or mother hen to many. I suppose that could be represented by the people, multiple nappies and the bees. 'Something missing', well, that rings true too; I intend to mother as many people as I can to fill this void within.

As for Mongolia, I have no idea what that is about, but I do know that it's a destination that I've been trying to get to for years. In my early twenties, I came close. I booked an overland trip through Mongolia along with my airfare—Australia, transiting China, then into Mongolia. Booked and deposit paid. Then one day, I noticed that my deposit had been refunded into my bank account. *Che cosa?* I called the travel agent, who told me that *I had called them a few weeks prior and cancelled the whole trip.* Something fishy was going on. SARS CoV-1 (an earlier coronavirus) was in full force during 2003, and China was experiencing the worst of it. I was comfortable with my plan to simply pass through China and move into the open space of Mongolia, but I had always suspected my mum was utterly uncomfortable with her little girl landing in an airport rampant with SARS. I took the refund and vowed I'd get to Mongolia some day.

Although I suspected that Mum may have been the one to cancel the trip, I never asked her about it. It may or may not have been her. I really have no idea. I could have asked. But there are times when I appreciate the practice of leaving the mysteries in life alone. There are so many things we cannot know, such as what will happen tomorrow, let alone bigger questions such as what happens in the afterlife. We can, of course, hold onto our personal beliefs and opinions which can provide security and perceived certainty to cling to, giving us some ease. But, really, none of us can be 100% sure that our beliefs are correct. That being the case, I feel it's important to find contentment in non-answers. In a way, this unanswered question of my Mongolia trip became my own private game, leaning into the not-knowing and forging a sense comfort in that.

I do hope to get to Mongolia one day. I'm not sure how this links in with me fulfilling my goal to mother one million people in my role as the queen bee. Perhaps that will be another unanswered question to carry forward with me into the future.

Update: My mum was the first person to read my freshly finished and unedited manuscript, including of course, this chapter. She called me after completing it, referred to this chapter, and announced "Sherrie, I would *never* do that! I may not agree with all of your decisions, but I will always support them."

Okay, so that answers that question. The mystery of who cancelled my trip remains. Perhaps it was simply an error on the part of the travel agent. Who knows?

Samatha and Vipassana

I wake up, cuddle the cat, and chat with Joel—him still in his wetsuit fresh from a surf, as I lie there in bed, waking up slowly. As Joel heads for the shower, I grab my bolster, my phone to use as a timer, and settle into position on the sheepskin rug for my morning meditation.

Lately, I've started running a script in my head. First, I focus on all the sounds I can hear, near and far, then I focus on my breathing until I realise that I'm distracted, no longer focused on my breathing, and I rein my attention back in (again and again). Next, I move into a visualisation, perhaps better described as kinaesthetic role play, imagining the osteoclasts (the cells in our body which degrade bone) removing the build-up of extra bone in the knuckle of my middle finger where the suggested arthritis is supposedly forming. I imagine my knuckle going back to its healthy state in 1994, before I had an accident with a coffee cup and ended up with multiple tiny shards of porcelain in my joint that the doctors couldn't retrieve.

I run this same script this morning. I feel my finger. I feel the knuckle. I imagine the osteoclasts working at it, reducing inflammation ... Then it dawns on me that the message this finger gave me in my first meditation, as it began to change, was that I needed to stop *doing, doing,* all the time. Here I am, in this meditation, fricking *doing*! Even in my meditation, the time and space I create for myself to *not do,* I am physically sitting in stillness yet mentally on task. *Stop it already!*

I'm half amused by my own antics and half excited by the realisation, but I'm wholly impressed by my ability to be self-aware enough to catch myself in the act, red-handed.

I stop with the osteoclasts. I come back to my breath. Inspired by my revelation, I have a new window of hope. If I can just stop *doing*, even if only in my meditations, my finger may settle back into normal movement and range of motion, without pain.

I breathe. I listen to sounds. I inhale ... exhale ...

My mind has run off again. Now it's mentally writing this whole narrative in words on a page. In my mind's eye, I can see a Word doc on my computer screen, with letters scrambling onto the page to download my mind's contents about what just happened. I realise that I'm writing this book—this paragraph!—mentally, in mid-meditation. Here I am, sitting, trying to be with my breath, letting go of focusing on my finger . . . letting go of the task to fix it, only to find that my mind is so excited by this latest revelation about me *doing*, that it gets busy writing the whole story down as it unfolds. *Now you're writing a book? Are you serious? STOP DOING!*

I pull myself back. I find my way to simply *be*.

Breathe . . . I feel the sensation of air moving in and out of my nose, passing over my throat, filling my lungs, my belly pushing outward . . . About one and a half breaths in, and I find the narrative is now being recited out loud to people, or to someone, in a conversation. I'm now imagining myself verbally sharing this whole story, from the beginning of the finger episode right up to mentally writing it all in my book. *Oh my God. Seriously? Breathe, Woman! Just breathe!*

Another fifteen seconds pass by.

I shift away from the Śamatha meditation style of consciously directing my focus (which is not my bag today, it seems), and into Vipassana, allowing my external environment to lead my focus. I allow my attention to organically move onto whatever my senses notice in each moment. I again tune in to all the sounds I can hear. There are birds outside my window. There's one bird that's not from around here. I haven't heard his song before. There are waves crashing against the cliff below. There are voices of those already up and going about their day. The foreign bird sings again. And I notice a tightness, a kind of dull ache, behind the bridge of my nose. I settle in there for a while, noticing what this dull ache feels like, just being with it. That strange bird again. I wonder what kind of bird it is and whether it's colourful or not. Then back to the heaviness in that feeling behind my nose.

My timer goes off. I stay here a while longer, feeling like I've only just started, then close my practice with my gratitude ritual. Thank you's are plentiful for my good night's sleep, my relationship with my husband, my husband himself, our home, my cat who goes out each night and chooses to come home to us again every morning. I am thankful for my health and for being alive at this time in the world—when Covid-19 has injected us into a surreal reality that feels like we're having our own Jumanji experience. I am thankful for the opportunities ahead to mother as many people as possible.

Mother's Day

Today is Mother's Day. The last few Mother's Days have made me cry. Not because I don't have cute little snotty things of my own cuddling me, but because I receive genuine heartfelt, heart-warming, tear-jerking Mother's Day messages. Lucy has sent me Mother's Day messages for the past few years, and they always bring tears to my eyes. In fact, the first one I received from her, telling me what a difference I'd made in her life, touched my heart so deeply it made me cry. Today, I also received a beautiful message from one of my clients:

> "Today is your day too. Happy Mother's Day, Sherrie.
> You, your teachings, your love, your support and your wisdom is what holds many of us motherless-mothers together.

I thank you xxx"

These words move me completely. I feel like I have mothered many already in my short time of 'being a mum,' so it's not that I *need* the recognition. But on this particular day, having people pause to acknowledge me as a mother figure is the most fulfilling, mind-blowing confirmation that *I'm doing it*. That I *am* a mother—my way.

In my daily meditations, up rises the conviction that I *will* ultimately mother one million people. Somehow. Some way—whether directly or indirectly.

And this is why I write.

I can now see how my training as a yoga teacher served to hold my hand and lead me to the keyboard under the guise of writing a book about yoga. I still occasionally make random notes for topics I want to include in that book, which may or may not ever see the light of day. However, I now appreciate that writing *that* book is what led to writing *this* book. And this book is where it's at for me. The recognition of this feels as real as anything I can reach out and touch. It is only in this moment I realise that this is the book I have been writing for years. This explains the feeling I used to have, while journaling, that the process had a far broader purpose than simply scribing my thoughts for my own sake. I just didn't know what that purpose was at the time. I see it now. This book is me sharing thoughts and life experiences, as any mother would, when speaking with their child, but on a grander scale as author to reader. It's a way for me to be the mother I've always known myself to be. This is me sharing thoughts in an effort to mentor, inspire and nurture. It's all on path. It feels so obvious to me now.

My first experience as a mother came in a furry, brown-and-white package — an eight-year-old ragdoll cat who spent years trawling our neighbourhood from apartment to apartment, scoring free meals and a place to sleep as his preference over going home. He would suffer bouts of fleas and ticks, and we would periodically take him to the vet and look after him in the absence of his owners doing the same. Eventually, they decided to officially give him away and his new owners moved him two suburbs away.

After roaming free for years, he was antsy as an inside cat. Twice, when the new owners let him outside, he smelled his way back to the headland where we live. After a long conversation with the new owners, who only had the cat's best interests at heart, we became his new, new owners. He was back on the headland and not surprisingly, once he had a home where he was loved, he stopped roaming the cul-de-sac. We watched him transition from street cat to the most gentle, beautiful little soul who just wanted to be near us. If we are working in the office, he curls up at our feet. If we are on the lounge, he is on the lounge. I've read that ragdoll cats are the most dog-like cats there are. I'm backing that up as truth. Ours even drools when he sleeps.

'Kitty' (his name stuck even after we found out that he was originally named Jonathan) made us a family of three. He runs around, full of energy, skidding along the wooden floors chasing his toys, then crashes out in the cutest pile of overgrown fluff. His body is only 10cm wide. His fur, however, grows up to 12cm long in winter, so he looks three times as big as his actual size.

The thing with Kitty, though, is not just about having a cat. It's having something to nurture, to love ... a little life in our home that allows us to witness each other as parents. I get to see my husband pandering to Kitty's every wish, and, in that way, I can see the dad within him. And, likewise, he sees me intuitively knowing what Kitty needs, that sometimes the only way he's going to settle is if you lie down with him for a few minutes. This little eight-year-old furball allows us not only to feel into our own parenting, but also to see each other as the kind of parents we are. Regardless of how different it might have been with children of our own, Kitty opened up a door for us to experience our version of parenting, and gradually, I found that the sadness from not knowing myself as a mum dissipated.

This parental position is occasionally amplified when our very fluffy kitty gets an upset stomach and subsequent diarrhoea. Gloved up and gasping for fresh air, it takes both Joel and I to clean him up, with Joel holding him and supporting his furry butt under the tap, and me washing him down—all while the little fur-bag is purring! I often laugh (retrospectively) at the parallel to new parents dealing with dirty nappies.

And, it may sound trivial, but when Kitty goes out each night around 1am, he comes back the next morning *to us*. When Joel opens the door at 4:30 in the morning (a stupid time to wake up, yet he does this daily regardless), Kitty is on our carpeted doorstep, curled up and waiting to be let back in. After experiencing the school pick up, where all these little humans ran around like mice, each homing in for their chosen parent, I now get to experience my version of being the one who is chosen. Every night, when Kitty goes out to roam his hood (or so we thought. It turns out he goes to the neighbour's apartment for a second dinner!), he could choose to go anywhere he wanted, and past experience showed him to be a capable street cat. But he chooses to come home to us.

It fills another hole of something I felt was missing.

Nothing has ever been missing, but the thought and feeling that something was missing was the catalyst which made me shift gear, making my time on earth feel that much more worthwhile and my contribution to humanity that much more refined.

Am I thankful for it? With my life.

Update

My middle finger is improving! The arthritis, if that's what it is, in the knuckle is starting to ease. The sensation is still there, but to such a lesser degree that the only way I know it's not completely healed is that it feels slightly bruised to touch. Other than that, I have full range of movement again. No pain and no discomfort.

So fascinating.

Meditation and Death

I pull my bolster out of the cupboard, grab my phone as a timer, and take a seat on my sheepskin rug. Kitty is on the bed next to me, watching with curiosity as I do a few seated stretches, moving my spine in all directions before I find centre and feel ready for meditation.

Sometimes I can spend the majority of my twenty-four-minute meditation in internal conflict about whether to stay seated or call it so I can go and do the seemingly urgent things harassing my thoughts, making me restless and unfocussed. Inevitably, I debate long enough until I exhaust the conversation and properly drop into a meditative state for the remaining time before my phone chimes. I'm always thankful that I stayed.

Today, I settle in effortlessly. Thoughts come and

it seems easy to recognise them and then park them, bringing my awareness back to the present moment. I notice the upright posture of my upper body and its weight grounding down into the bolster. I notice my folded legs and the sounds of the waves crashing outside, a constant rumble. I listen to the sounds of my cat licking and cleaning himself next to me. A key unlocks our front door. Joel is home from surfing. I hear him walk past the bedroom door behind me. The sound of the shower. I drink in all the sounds, just listening in absolute presence to my current experience.

My mind momentarily takes me forward in time, asking me to recognise that, one day, I may sit here without the sound of my cat or my husband. I mentally acknowledge the impermanent nature of all things. I can always find my way back to ocean sounds, but there may come a day when I don't have the beings most precious to me by my side. I take in this moment I have right now. The perfection of it. I recognise that, while my external world will continue to alter moment-to-moment, there is something within the essence of who I am which remains constant and unchanging. This part of me remains present to all the content of my life and looks on as a spectator, enjoying the show. This part of me, awareness itself, always watches on, unaffected by the changing acts on the stage. There are characters playing happy, sad, friendly and angry roles. There are highs and lows to keep the show dynamic, each scene flowing naturally into the next. Death is part of the show. It's part of every show. So, I wait, I look on. I anticipate it with curiosity, wondering how I will move through that scene when it comes.

For years, I have had an acute sense of the impending death of those around me. I feel like I've spent many years preparing for the death of loved ones. I remember long ago visiting my grandmother at her home, and every time I said goodbye, I'd drive away with tears welling, wondering if I'd ever see her again. It would be another twelve years before she passed and, in that time, I became very practised at anticipating her death.

It has become my way of being to hold one eye on the very vivid reality that I may never see someone again. I am constantly feeling into the last goodbye, every time. I feel its weight each time my husband goes for a surf. Without fail, when I say, "Have fun, Bino," my words are accompanied by a feeling of potential finality. Time slows down, my heart opens and I become acutely aware of the love we share. *Take this moment in. It may be your parting memory of him.*

I am certain that this, perhaps morbid, undercurrent in my thinking is one of my major contributions to making our relationship as strong as it is. When you realise that you don't know how much time you have to spend with someone you love, you cherish every moment. It's the uncertainty factor. If I think I will have him with me for another fifty years, I might take today for granted. I might take Joel for granted. Yet, when I consider that, for all we know, we may only have three days left together, I honour every moment we have to love and appreciate one another. And that's not to demand he stay by my side every minute. Rather, I respect the need for each of us to spend our time doing something we find fulfilling. Sometimes this means we travel overseas without each other. Sometimes it means we go on long road trips together where we spend the first few days picking off every thought from the low-hanging branches of our psyche. By the fourth day of staring at highways, dirt roads and long horizons, having bled out all superficial thoughts and idle conversation, we unleash deeper sentiments that we didn't even know were in there as unbirthed thoughts. We road trip well together. The silence. The chit chat. The life-changing conversations. The whole journey we take together. It feels like really living. And when I feel that we truly are *living* each moment, I find more peace with the knowledge that one day death will have its moment too.

I know it's coming. And I wait, perhaps with an overzealous focus, while experiencing an enriched marriage in real-time, purely on the basis that I don't take Joel for granted.

Game of Lego

It was a week ago that I finished writing the last chapter about my quiet anticipation of others' deaths. Two days ago, I found out about a friend's death. His was not one I'd practised for.

I hadn't seen Andy G in three years. I worked for him for eight years until he sold the company from which I was later made redundant. It's been thirteen years since I worked for him and our catch ups were intermittent after that—once every couple of years or so. Although he hadn't physically been in my life for the past few years, the news of his death rocked me. Perhaps driven by my closet fascination with death, I am just as fascinated by my response—two days of intermittent tears for somebody I haven't seen in years.

On day two of crying, I realise that I'm not crying over his death. What I'm realising is that Andy G's death allowed me to wholly recognise the enormous impact he had on my life. The news crystallised my understanding and incredibly deep gratitude for where I am in life, largely thanks to Andy G. Andy G stood out by a mile—ten miles—in comparison with my previous employers. Where they marked out a steep divide between themselves and me, as their dispensable employee, Andrew treated me like a valued person. In fact, he was the first adult outside of my family who spoke with me like my brain and my contribution were highly valued. He made me feel that I had value, just the way I was. In contrast to employers who seemed to value me based on my potential to be something good (one day), Andy G made me feel like I was already something good. He promoted me into various roles because he believed in my capacity to expand into them. And because of that, I flourished. It was under Andy G's wing that I found my feet as an adult—and my own wings. It was on his watch that I toyed with personal boundaries and glass ceilings, all of them shattering as I grew into a self-respecting, strong and independent female. My mum has well and truly role modelled this behaviour ever since I can remember, so I knew what it looked like from the outside, but here I was given an opportunity to find it within me. When I pause to consider my life trajectory before versus after meeting Andy G, I feel every part of me beaming with gratitude for this person. He was certainly an enormous gift to me, and now all I can do is feel these tears rolling down my cheeks in overwhelming gratitude.

    I turn to my sheepskin rug. I lower myself down

onto the bolster and close my eyes to go inward. I drop into meditation easily today and, almost immediately, I watch as a scene unfolds in my mind's eye.

There's a young girl. She's playing with her Lego set. She has a large quantity of lego men, women and children all spread out for her game, each with a different hat on, or different hair or eye colour, different clothing—something to differentiate them from each other. She picks them up individually, bringing the pieces onto the centre stage where she acts out various scenes, putting on different voices and accents for each piece. Some of the scenes are beautiful and harmonious. Some scenes are aggressive with wars being played out, individuals arguing and yelling, sometimes dying. The sound effects that go with the death scenes are that of a child's make-believe game, dramatic and full of imagination. As the lego people die, she removes them from the game and tosses them to the side with a lack of emotion.

With her now-free hand, the little girl simply reaches for another piece to bring onto the stage and a new voice with corresponding accent is now in motion. The remaining lego family related to the lego person who died are all pushed together in a huddle. Different voices of 'there there' are offered up, along with intermittent cries, hugs and wailing. Once the funeral and the mourning are done, the little girl moves all the people on in their lego lives to keep the game moving forward.

Some people hold the belief that we are all one. This concept of oneness resembles the little girl's game in my meditation. One little girl plays every role in the game, pretending to be multiple people, but really, they are all her. At their source, all the lego people in the game are only one person. Andy G had been removed from the game, but was he truly gone? How do you define 'gone' if the essence, the common denominator of each character, is just a little girl throwing her voice? In this game, the little girl *is* Andy G. And she didn't go anywhere. She's still playing. She is playing every single role.

Lego people come and go in her game, moving through the motions of harmony and laughter and struggle and loss in their lego lives. Yet, the little girl playing out these individual roles, the one who *is* each of us, remains constant throughout. She *is* the unchanging awareness. And she's still playing. She's there putting on accents and loaning lego pieces personality. There is no death, per se, in her make-believe game. There is simply role playing with different characters moving on and off stage over the course of time.

And the game, it continues. Wars, famines, floods, fires, Covid-19, protests, festivals, weddings, divorces, global meditations . . . death, birth, death, birth . . . the game plays on. All the while, the little girl, this master controller, is both captivated and inspired by her dynamic and exciting game.

Lego Practice

The game of lego continues to play out in my mind. And thankfully, too. A lady, maybe thirty-years-old, comes to my first yoga class after the studios reopen following the Covid-19 isolation period. She pulls me aside to update me on her personal situation. She takes a deep breath, pauses for a moment to hold herself together, and tells me that her mum had an accident and recently passed away. She lets me know that she's feeling emotionally fragile and may become upset during class. As she's telling me this, I feel a bulge in my throat and tears start welling up. An instinctive return to the lego game allows me to pull myself together. I see the little girl playing her game with lego Mum and lego daughter and their whole lego family. For reasons unknown to the individual lego pieces, it's time for lego Mum to leave the game, and so her exit is played out with her piece removed from centre stage. The remaining lego family are gathered into a huddle.

This split-second scene allows me to maintain composure and be able to support this beautiful girl, rather than be the one blubbering on her shoulder for her loss. *There is no loss.* The perceived loss is in our little plastic lego heads. But there is no loss.

I am quietly thankful for the role-playing practice I'm receiving, knowing that when it comes my time to mourn a loved one, the perceptions in my little yellow[*] plastic lego head are going to swell to all-consuming levels, as if the loss were real. I am aware of this and, at the same time, feel into this new idea of the little girl and her game, which feels even more real at this moment. I feel her fingers around me, moving my lego life from one conversation to the next. Always supported…always held. Never alone.

---

[*] During the initial wave of Covid-19, when businesses all over the world converted their products and services into an online offering, I sat in on a live-streamed human dissection by anatomist and 'somanaut' Gil Hedley. I appreciated the way he idolised human form—in all its uniqueness and wonder. The first layer to be removed is obviously the skin. Watching this, I wished everybody could have seen and heard his demonstration. This superficial layer was removed to show the fascia and adipose tissue (fat layer) beneath the surface, the yellow tissue just a millimetre or so under the skin.

Below the surface layer of every human being, regardless of how light, medium or dark the pigmentation of their skin, we are all yellow. Humans are yellow, with just a thin layer of pigmented skin on top. And below the yellow, we're pink and red and bits of blue. We're actually a beautiful rainbow of colour—all of us.

Recalling Gil's words, I giggle to myself when I realise that the original lego pieces were all yellow. Lego pieces were unrelatable to any realistic human skin colour. However, this generic colour chosen is actually the closest to the truth for representing the human race.

The Shift

Now that a few months have passed since my brother's surgery, I am aware that something has shifted between us. Our relationship has matured. I never expected this change, nor did I ever think that our relationship should change, but it most definitely has. We've always been close and have adored each other since he, as a toddler, held his brand-new baby sister. As the younger sibling, I grew up idolising my big brother. And although he was my older brother, I often felt that I took on the elder sibling role when it came to emotional strength. I remember one night, our parents went out for dinner while Shane and I stayed at home with our grandmother. Shane was crying as he watched them leave because he didn't want them to go. I distinctly remember trying to comfort him by saying, "They'll be back soon, it's only dinner and then they'll be home again". Perhaps that was when I first became a mother.

For me, this motherly feeling toward him remained as we moved through our teenage years and into our twenties. I comforted him through each of his broken romantic relationships and, sadly, through the loss of friends to suicide. These roles remained into our thirties. I was the go-to person for emotionally difficult topics and served as the shoulder of support. We continued in the same vein into our forties, until that day at the hospital. I didn't realise at the time just how pivotal that moment, pre-surgery, would be for us. While he was in his blue gown pretending to listen to the nurse's instructions, he was focusing on me instead. I remember he nodded and gave a vague "yep" to the nurse, then turned straight back toward me with a look of concern—for *me*. I had become inconsolable. And in that moment, there was a shift taking place. I was able to see the true capacity of his emotional strength. He personified it.

It took me a few months, and resuming my 'normal' way of life, to recognise that this was not the same version of life I had known. This was a new normal. The dynamics between Shane and me have changed. Both of us now in our forties, it feels like the playing field has levelled. We have finally come to a place of brother and sister—no longer big brother, little sister, nor me taking on a big sister role looking after my brother's heart. We both have the capacity to support each other and know that the other person is strong enough to also support themselves. As somebody who cares so deeply for this other human and his whole experience in life, this change for me—this relief from worry—has huge consequences in my life.

It's the mother in me. I recognise it. From being that little kid who comforted Shane when Mum and Dad went out, to growing up and being his nurturer, this has been my way of being. I can see how, all along, he has been fundamental to knowing myself in the mothering role. I come back to the realisation that nothing is ever missing. And now, even as I watch him step out from under my wing and hold his own, I feel my own version of experiencing a child growing up and moving out of home. I get it. That feeling that mothers must have after looking out for someone 24/7, only to come to a time when you see your baby all grown up and making their own decisions that inspire you, holding themselves in a way that you could never do *for* them. I feel my compulsion to worry about him quieten, my headspace become a little freer, and my heart become filled with even more love and inspiration for him, and *because of* him.

I gently move through all the feelings of motherhood, and I am eternally thankful to my brother for his gift of being exactly who he is.

Vantage Point

The lego game never wanders far from my thoughts these days, even interrupting my morning gratitude ritual. Every morning, before I get out of bed, I first acknowledge what I am thankful for. I then consider my day ahead and become thankful, in advance, for opportunities coming up that day. This practice seamlessly doubles as a kind of intention-setting for me. Today, as I consider all the upcoming opportunities I'm thankful for, I realise that what I am mentally cycling through is more like a to-do list than a gratitude list, with me simply imagining how I'd like to see them all play out.

In many ways, I believe there's just as much to be learned and gained from so-called mundane life as from walking the spiritual path. Yet, this morning, I question myself, the little girl's voice in my head, ever-present and spurring me on. *Is the most effective way to spend my time today simply to move through my to-do list? And did I create this list, or did somebody else create it for me and I simply agreed, in exchange for income or something? Is there a greater contribution I could be making today with my time? What will* actually *bring me closer to my goal of mothering one million people? Surely these twenty-four hours should count toward something. And if they don't, how many other twenty-four-hour periods have I disregarded as an opportunity to reach my goals? What will make today count?*

I lie in bed a little longer, considering a bigger picture. I try to hold the broader perspective seen by the little girl. More and more, I gain insight and direction from my meditations. It doesn't happen like that every day; however, the daily meditation practice provides me with epiphanies regularly enough to truly appreciate its value. It helps to light my way on this path and foster a deeper understanding of myself.

So, I get up out of bed and I sit. Settling onto my bolster to meditate, soon, all I am aware of is the soundtrack of the moment. The ocean, rumbling and crashing against the cliff... voices in the street, a car starting, the sounds of community ... background noises coming from the kitchen—the clinking of Joel's spoon stirring his cup of tea ... the purring next to me, intermittently dispersed with the strange and beautiful bird-like noises that my cat makes, as he too sets himself up for the day.

The little girl, playing her game of lego. Me, the lego piece, talking and interacting with other lego pieces. My sense of clarity around this scenario grows day by day. I know the little girl is me. The me that I think I am *is* the little girl acting out a Sherrie role on the game board, with a Sherrie voice and a Sherrie accent, but I'm all her.

I feel her close. Her thumb and first finger around my lego body lift me up to a vantage point where I join her in watching the whole game play out below. I visually take in the entire game board—all of life on earth. And yet, even whilst I soak up this grand view, maintaining awareness that *this is* the game of life, I remain as a lego piece. She can lift me up so I can see; however, my perceptions of this game are confined by the limitations that come with being a lego piece on the game board. I may have glimpses of a broader awareness, but my understanding remains filtered through the eyes of a lego piece.

What will make today count? I mentally come back to this book. In many ways, this book feels more real than anything else I could create as a means of mothering. Writing this book today will make today count. Then I revisit the idea of doing a neuroscience degree. I've arrived at a place in my mind where I make no distinction between science and (my version of) spirituality. For me, they are different languages which ultimately speak of the same wild phenomenon that is life. I spent many years investigating spirituality, and now I'm ready to further my scientific understanding. I submitted my application for university just recently and am waiting to hear back. This also feels right to me. The ten-year vision board I created during the last week of 2019 includes a graduation picture. It represents me obtaining a Human Sciences degree within this 2020-2029 decade.

With this clarification on what will actually make today count, I redesign my day and prioritise these things. What else do I need to do to prepare for university, knowing that this week I will find out if I have been accepted, and, if so, the semester starts on Monday? Today, I will prioritise my life around that, as if it is already written that I have been accepted. This means re-working my calendar to schedule in enough time to write as well, regardless of other people's requests of me and regardless of university. This book is my priority.

And now that I have my day planned *for me*, I am truly thankful for the opportunities coming up and that *today* takes me one step closer to mothering one million people. My heart full of gratitude, I'm ready for today.

Beyond Purpose

I remember a kinesiology session I had last year. I left the session quite confused, even a little annoyed. The line of questioning from the practitioner felt like an attempt to fracture the foundation I had built my life on.

Every therapist I've worked with loves to drill down on the fact that I can't bear children, and wants to dig around for dark emotional leftovers from this experience. In this kinesiology appointment, I was very direct and as articulate as I could be in explaining that I have found this aspect of my life to be a blessing, that I see the whole experience as a gift.

She wasn't having it.

> I try again. "This supposed 'void' *is* what drives me. This experience shone the light on my purpose—with incredible clarity! Whereas

before, I moved through life ticking boxes, now I am utterly lit up on the inside."

"But who are you without this? Who are you if you're not a mother?"

WTF. "No, no . . . I am a mother. That is me. That is who I am."

"Sure, but what are you under that, outside of that, without that?"

What?

Only now do I appreciate where she was going with her line of questioning. She wanted me to realise that any label I identified with was simply that—a label. She wanted me to see that I was more than that. What feels enormous to me—to feel with absolute certainty that I *am* a mother, to mother one million people—all pales when I look at it from the broader view of the game. I'm not (just!) a mother, I am also the little girl. The little girl plays more than one role. She plays every role. She's the mother, as well as the child being mothered. She's the dog she makes barking noises for, she's the tree that shakes in the wind that she blows with her breath. She's the homeless person, the bank teller, the pharmacist, and the pilot. She's everyone. If I am she, I am everyone. I am far grander than *just* a mother. And yet, thanks to this gift of my confined lego perception, I am able to feel a deep yearning rooted within—as if something is missing. It is this yearning which lights the fire of motivation in me, continually driving me to seek ways to feel fulfilled.

This *is* what stretches me to grow.

If it weren't for my lego attributes, if I felt a perfect sense of wholeness already, then inertia may set in. Why would I do anything at all? Would there even be anything to do? It is my lego-ness which creates the sense of void and causes me to perceive something as missing. This *is* the drive. This *is* what sets the game in motion. This is the momentum that gives life to our whole existence.

The broader view from the Vantage Point gives us understanding, but the lego factor gives us drive. Sensing lack, loss, desire, goals and accomplishments . . . all of these things give rise to our sense of purpose. All of these aspects give movement to these otherwise static yellow bodies, and become the very ingredients which allow us to experience life. What an overwhelming gift. This gift allows us to temporarily suspend our full capacity of understanding the lego game.

Instead, we play out melodramatic roles of grand love, affection, addiction, fear and loss, make-believe deadlines, huge decisions, all the highs, all the lows . . . and we live them like they're real. We play like this game is life itself. What a magical experience to have, all the while appreciating, on a very deep and hidden level, that we are the little girl playing all roles at the same time, owning the whole game.

Mindset

I've been accepted into university. I spend Thursday to Sunday trying to navigate the university website, along with the various online learning platforms that we're dependent on in this Covid-19 era. I keep tweaking the timetables of my enrolled units until I can fit everything in—lectures, tutorials, reading, studying, assignments, writing this book, teaching yoga, some social time, some eating time, all the while maintaining lots of sleep—my non-negotiable.

The degree I'm starting, a Bachelor of Cognitive and Brain Science, is a three-year degree, full time, or six years, part time. The deal I made with myself when considering studying was that it had to be balanced in such a way that *I can do everything*—write, earn, learn—without burning out. The way I work it out, this will have me graduating in around four and a half years, meaning

I will still be able to honour the plan Joel and I made to move out of Sydney in four to five years' time.

Approaching the end of my second week in, my emotional resilience has already been tested. The first week's workload lulled me into a false sense of ease, before moving into full throttle this week. Today's line-up was a full day of studying, attending lectures, studying, preparing a yoga class, time to eat, then heading off to teach yoga at night. Joel won't be home until late, so I'm on my own for cooking as well. As the evening arrived, work time for me had run out and I needed to be in the kitchen already. I felt the stress rise.

One shouldn't use a sharp knife when feeling stressed and rushed. I learned this today. University has already served me well, and I am now wiser than I was before I made dinner.

I pulled myself up and came back to my mantra: *I can do everything*. It's just a simple statement, yet one that has a substantial impact on my underlying attitude. As soon as I reminded myself of this deal I had made, it was as if I imagined myself as someone who literally could do everything I wanted to, with ease. It completely changed the way I related to the moment. I imagined myself as someone who could float through all tasks, actioning them one by one, with every task having its own dedicated time and space. There was no rush. There was time for everything. There *is* time for everything. I *am* that person. I *can* do everything.

A sense of calm comes over me and shifts my whole state of being. I realise that I grew up practising the habit of stressing. If I was in a rush, I'd throw stress on top of it. If I was feeling busy and my schedule was full, I'd add stress as a bonus ingredient into the mix. However, if I am choosing to be a person who can do everything, then there's no need for the additional ingredient. Rather, I can simply move through one task at a time.

There is an instant calm.

I've been reminding myself of this mantra every day since then, and it allows me to feel not only comfortable with my workload, but inspired by the prospect of being that person who can do it all—*and* enjoy the process. I feel a fire light in my belly. I can do it all.

This morning, I wake and begin writing straight after my meditation. My mum, not knowing whether I am interruptible, but wanting to check in on me all the same, sends me a text message to see how I'm going with my university workload. I pause from writing and send her a quick reply:

> "So far, so good. I'm just having a book-writing session at the moment. The aim is to do everything :)"

> "Just as well that 'everything' is possible."

Her reply is more than perfect. I can't imagine a more supportive and elevating confirmation of her belief in my ability to achieve this—all of this.

My mind wanders back to the little girl. She moves

me from one task to the next. She's not in a hurry. It's just a game. She's making all the rules, and she owns the timing of each move made. She holds both my lego body and the body of my lego mum, and nods each of their heads in the gesture of two pieces in conversation. She uses lego mum to reassure lego me that everything is possible. She's got this game covered.

I come back to my book.

Wendy

Sometimes, in my rambling thoughts, I jokingly and affectionately refer to the little girl as *Wendy*. It's a throwback to when I was about four years old and appeared on a television show called *Romper Room*, featuring a panel of preschoolers. The host, Miss Helena, would introduce each of the six kids for their televised 'show and tell', before all sorts of games began.

One of the games included a felt-covered board, on which we had to stick a variety of little felt cut-out pieces. This is where I met Wendy. Wendy was one of the cut-outs. There was also a hose and a shovel and other gardening implements. The felt background was Wendy's garden, and I was nominated to dress Wendy and set her up in her garden, sticking all the felt pieces into place. Miss Helena corrected me a couple of times for putting a piece in the wrong place, such as the rolled-up hose standing vertically in the sky. Other than these corrections, I created Wendy's world. Wendy may have thought that she was in charge of her felt life and her felt garden, but I was the little girl who was moving all the pieces around and creating Wendy's world. And now that I can identify with being the felt piece, and have a sense that someone else is the little girl moving all the pieces of my life into place, I affectionately refer to this little girl as Wendy, in some sort of cute role reversal.

All the while I do this, I remind myself not to fall into the habit of personifying her too much. 'The little girl' is a metaphor and a metaphor only. 'She' is not a girl, she's not a person, and she doesn't have a personality. However, it's difficult for people to refer to non-tangible, invisible things without feeling compelled to attribute human traits to it—purely for the sake of providing the unknown with a level of comfort and familiarity. Some religions embrace the concept that man makes God in his own image. Admittedly, this phrase is generally stated in reverse: God made man in his own image, but I've always thought the former, personified version felt more accurate. Human brains don't like stories without endings, or questions without answers. We will hypothesise, consciously or unconsciously, and use our imagination to make something up if we need to, simply to provide some relief and closure for our gasping brains. I believe it's likely that this innate habit of making something in *our* own image, which is otherwise so incomprehensible, is what allows us to wrap our head around it as best we can.

It's our attempt to make sense of what we don't know at an intellectual or factual level. It is the concept of the little girl lifting me up to the Vantage Point and, although I can then see the whole game with her broad perspective, I remain limited to only being able to perceive that view with my lego mind—because that's what I'm here with. That is the only way the game can be played. Lego pieces must be lego. Because if we all knew that we were Wendy, then there would be no 'other' people in this world, just Wendy—on her own. Without lego, there is no game. Yet, if our thinking is limited in a way that means we perceive ourselves as individuals, then we can function as a society of many. And so lego pieces must play as lego, within these confines of lego limitations.

There's a philosophical question as to whether humans have the capacity to think on behalf of any other living thing. Can we think on behalf of nature, to make the best decisions on how to treat the environment, when we are limited by a human-thinking mind? Can we truly think on the same scale as a river, if making decisions for that river? Do we know enough to appreciate all of the intricate nuances of the river and how it is impacted by and impacts the multitude of relationships it has with the rocks, the soil, the sea life, atmosphere, the algae, all flora and fauna, the mountaintop, flood-lands, grasses and lakes? With the best of intentions, we can make decisions with what we know, but what about the potential plethora of facts that we don't know we don't know. How do we account for that?

Since I can only think within the limited capacity of my mind, like the metaphorical lego piece that I am, I am aware that it's more comfortable for me to give 'Wendy' a name to personify her. When people choose to personify some sort of divine order, it allows them to better relate to it and even speak directly with it (via prayer) in the same way we would speak with another person. In those conversations, we can ask questions and make requests. We can tell 'her' what we don't like, and thank her for all we do like. We can even imagine her judging us from above—passing judgements which are, coincidentally, an exact reflection of our own judgements.

I lovingly call her Wendy, with a smile and giggle each time. There is no character called Wendy, and she's not a little girl. She's a metaphor. Wendy represents the base ingredient that makes up all life, that which *is* life. She is prime matter, the connection between all things. She appeared in my meditation in the form of a little girl to help me make sense of my experiences and process my emotions and thoughts. And *she* has had a huge impact on the way I have processed my experiences since then. Yet the little girl is simply a metaphor for the totality of this grand network of life on Earth.

If we are limited by the capacity of our lego mind, it may be more natural to think in terms of one lego lifetime, rather than to think holistically, and view the entire game. This is not just one round marked by the beginning and end of our own lifetime, but a whole continuous, perhaps timeless, game. We are all one and the same. We are like the river in that sense, one perfectly working system full of intricate nuances which impact and are impacted by all of the seen and unseen relationships we have with every other living thing—every other component of this game. This is where the metaphor of Wendy comes in. It's a way to wrap my head around the enormity of my life, beyond the plastic boundaries of my own yellow body. I am Wendy. She is me. She is every other lego piece which means I am also every other lego piece. There is no separation. There is no beginning and end of a lego life in this view. There is one game, and we are every piece on the board. We are the game—in continuous motion. Each single experience aids the direction of the game. There is no experience which is not worthy.

And so, now that I have this comprehensible lego metaphor for my mind to grasp, I internally smile at Wendy, thanking her for leading me down this path and connecting the dots for me like she does.

Being Whole

As I continue contemplating this idea of Wendy, it occurs to me that for her to play every role on the game board, she must first have the capacity to think and feel in all the different ways being played out in the game. If Wendy is not familiar with the feeling of sadness, then she will never be able to play a sad role with any of her pieces. In fact, it wouldn't even occur to her to have a sad lego piece as this emotion is not within her sphere of awareness. Wendy can only express the emotions and traits within her. All emotions and traits played in the game are therefore emotions and traits of Wendy. This includes every single act, emotion and thought that any lego piece on the board is doing, feeling or thinking. This includes the whole range of experiences, extending to the very edges of the spectrum. If something is not part of Wendy, it simply cannot be played out in her game.

I sit with this concept.

Every role played on this game board comes from a pool of possibilities within Wendy. Every emotion portrayed by the multitude of lego pieces is an emotion realised within Wendy. Every thought these lego pieces have, every word they say, and every action they make comes from within Wendy because she is the one playing this game. She welcomes every part of herself into the game. She restricts nothing. It's 'game on' and every aspect of her is involved.

If Wendy plays the part of every lego piece, this means that each individual piece possesses every trait played on this game board. We are each whole. We have every trait within us. So even if we are currently playing the role of a kind and friendly lego piece, we also have unkind traits within us. Yet, when we see unkind traits in another, we will often shun both the traits and the other person, shocked that someone could act in such an unkind way. Whereas Wendy experiences no degree of difference when playing one lego piece or the other.

Every trait or characteristic that we see in other people is also within ourselves. We play out these traits differently to other people and that's how the game remains dynamic and sustains momentum.

This concept... I've been here before. At the height of my transition phase, when I was moving from yearning to be a mother to appreciating that I already was a mother, this was the broader perspective I sought. I needed to find where I already owned this mothering trait and how it was showing up in my life, with the understanding that it simply must be present within me, by 'universal' (Wendy's) law.

The exercise I took myself through was designed to consciously expose the fact that nothing was missing; that I was already whole. It was this effort I sat with when I asked myself, *If mothering is present within me, and is not missing, then where and how is it being played out?* To find it and recognise it in my life was the only way to *know* it was already present. This was how I came to realise that I was already nurturing others. I was already mothering by mentoring, teaching, cooking, and even cleaning up after others in the act of cleaning my cat's furry butt—my nappy-changing equivalent. As a result of this exercise, I was able to recognise that the version of motherhood that appeared in the brochure was only missing from my life when viewed through the narrow lenses of my lego eyes. From the broader perspective, I found motherhood to be present in my own version of it.

I am familiar with this Vantage Point and accept the reality that nothing is missing within us. I hold this truth within me. I live this knowledge.

And now, I find myself back in this contemplative space to confirm that nothing is missing. Yet, this time, I'm coming from the other direction. Previously I attempted to fill my motherhood gap so I could feel whole. Today, through the metaphor of Wendy, I start with the understanding that every human is already whole.

With rich clarity, maintained in the present

moment, I consider wars. I consider all the horrific things that happen all over the globe. I have found that our experiences cannot be labelled good or bad as a binary judgement. Rather, every experience has both benefits and drawbacks, when seen from different perspectives—and when viewed from the Vantage Point.

Thanks to my newly clarified concept of Wendy, I have a broader perspective from which to consider my reality. With this metaphor of Wendy, I understand how we each have all traits. Nothing is ever missing in us. Yet it remains true that we perceive there is. With our five senses and our limited perspective, we experience that the things we desire most and do not have are undeniably missing from our life. Then we bag up the despised traits of others, and like to imagine that we don't have them either.

Other people are bad, we are good. It's these limited perspectives which create inner conflict by denying half of who we really are. If we wish to live a wholesome and fulfilling life, yet shun parts of ourselves, suppressing them and pretending that those parts do not exist, then is it any surprise that we do this to other people? Is it any surprise that we shun others, aiming to suppress them and their ways? We quash our own disliked parts the same way we aim to quash people who do not support our cause, our belief, or our way of life. Any news channel offers real-time examples of the human preference to silence or even remove 'other' pieces from the game.

The Dalai Lama purportedly said, "We can never obtain peace in the outer world until we make peace with ourselves." This is a beautiful teaching and worthy of consideration. Yet, like many wise words, it is at risk of being converted into a cliché by those catering to the two-second attention span of people scrolling through social media. All too easily, spiritual wisdom like this becomes another generic meme forwarded around the planet daily. *Bla bla . . . something spiritual . . . add love.* Got it.

When I consider this quote again now, I realise how outer wars are also inner wars. Why do we make war with each other? Because we have wars within. We prefer to reject parts of who we are, rather than claim our disliked parts. We have conflict within, so we have conflict in our life. Fighting with someone else represents, and actually *is*, fighting with ourselves. There is no separation between our outer world and our inner world. To hate parts of ourselves is to be at war with parts of humanity. To hate any other human is to hate a part of yourself. I understood the words of Dalai Lama intellectually, but now I understand it as embodied knowledge.

To love ourselves, to accept all parts of ourselves, to embrace the good, the bad and the ugly within us, *is* to stop the wars. To end war, we must each find peace within ourselves—because those on the 'outside', against whom we wage war, are just other parts of ourselves. If we are all one and the same, the superficial yellow plastic which distinguishes your lego arm from my lego arm is solely for the purposes of our game. We are one and the same. I am you. You are me. We are not separate, save these distinguishing features of our lego bodies, animated purely for the purpose of having a game with more than one character on the board.

If we can make peace with every aspect of ourselves, wholeheartedly accepting every single part of us, this is to love one another. To end the conflict within is the only way to end the conflict.

Love

I was distracted this morning in my meditation. My thoughts were focused on the younger version of me appearing on *Romper Room*. Little Sherrie, dressed in blue, with long brunette hair and an oversized pink bangle. I was shy until I was about fourteen, which was when I began to question everything about the world and the people in it, as well as why I would give their opinions so much weight. I now understand that this is the age when people commonly question society and buck boundaries as they transition into adulthood. Yet, as this little four-year-old dressed in blue, I was still very shy.

My actual memories of being on *Romper Room* are minimal. However, I have footage of the show on a digital file that fills in the blanks. Watching the show makes my heart smile each time. I look at this little girl likely the way a mother would look at her own child. I see this little thing that looks like me, a younger version of me, yet I don't know what thoughts are going through her head. I don't recall her full experience of the moment. I am more of a bystander watching her live this experience. She feels quite distant from who I am now, so I really don't relate to her as being me. She's just a little girl who looks like me. I think that is the reason I gaze at her so lovingly. She could be my daughter.

I look at her little hands, so perfect as they fumble with her balloon in one of the games they played. Her little face, pondering and impressed by the other kids' show-and-tell craftsmanship. I watch her face as she wants to say something when she misses out in Musical Chairs, but is too shy to speak up. My heart swells. I love watching her take in life, each moment new to her, just figuring it out as she goes along. *You can't get it wrong baby girl, it's the first time you've ever lived* this *moment. Just be you. You're perfect.*

It's so fascinating to feel this depth of love for myself *only* when I can separate myself from my own self-judgement. When I can create enough distance to no longer relate to myself as self, then I can wholeheartedly appreciate the perfection of this human moving through life with all the awkwardness of someone who is unrehearsed for each new moment. The fact that she placed Wendy's hose sideways on the board fills my heart, knowing she's doing what she thinks is best, based on what she knows about the world so far. I love the fact that she forgot the name of the flowers that she brought for show-and-tell, despite my mum helping me practice "wattle" all the way there in the car.

It's her way of being that makes her adorable. It's her humanness. Watching her think through situations and wondering how she'll react. Her ways, her pure rawness, her idiosyncrasies, they all make her loveable. They make her relatable and real—and gorgeous. They give her personality and depth and create situations where she needs to respond to consequences, and it's this that I love to watch. It's the way she intuitively responds to life, to an environment that she can't always predict and can't control, and it's this that I fall in love with. Her. This perfect human.

To love the forty-two-year-old version of me in the same way . . . to end the self-deprecating talk that rumbles internally. To end the internal conflict. To end the wars. It feels like an impossible task. Of course, it is possible (presumably?), but it feels like the biggest challenge we humans could face in our existence. Self-love without constraint. Perhaps that is the journey for each of us. Perhaps the overarching purpose of every lived experience on earth is to find a way to feel love for ourselves without hidden clauses and exclusion zones. Maybe we're collectively going through eight billion various experiences, each of them making up the Whole (with a capital W, analogous to Wendy's W), to be whole, to feel whole . . . to play out every role and collectively experience wholeness. Every aspect of Wendy, collectively alive, lived, experienced . . . appreciated, loved. The near-impossible task of accepting ourselves as we are, lovingly, in order to own and experience this wholeness within.

Could it be possible to do such a thing? Can we love ourselves without boundaries?

I feel my eyes becoming sleepy, so I park my thoughts of love, put my book down and turn off my bedside lamp. The change in light, or perhaps the sound of the light switch, wakes Joel out of the early stages of sleep. He opens up his arms, reaching both in my direction. As I roll into them, he pulls my body on top of his. The top of my head nestles into his shoulder, and under my cheek, I feel the rise and fall of his chest with every breath he breathes, filling up this intermittent space between us.

Eventually I make small kisses on his shoulder, an indication I will soon roll onto my side of the bed to fall asleep for the night. One word, gently whispered…

"*Stay.*"

And I do.

In the morning, we wake to our tenth wedding anniversary. Joel and I remarry each other every five years, so while today is our tenth anniversary, it's also our third wedding. The first one was the legal marriage, and so we no longer need licensed celebrants to hold our ceremonies. The five-year ceremonies are about creating a space for reflection on who we each are now, who we are as a couple, and what we want to aim toward going into the next five years. It's to consciously press the pause button on life to recognise that I've changed, you've changed, we've changed . . . and I still choose you.

A few nights ago, after one of our epic roast vegetable dinners, we set ourselves up on the couch with two cups of tea, a block of dark chocolate and our wedding vows.

I promise to love you for who you are
and give you freedom to grow.
I promise to support you, to be your best friend
and to always build our world together.
I will make you tea and always enjoy our life together.
I offer my trust, my future,
my love, my honesty
and my word that we will always share the fun times
and support each other in times of need.
I offer this to you and only you, now and always.

We re-read these original vows, recognising how much more deeply we know each other now compared to when we wrote them over ten years ago. Then come the additions—the 'addendums', as we refer to them. The first addendum is our vows from our second wedding in 2015.

I promise to cheers forks.
And all I know is that there is nothing better,
nothing stronger, nothing more loving
and nothing funnier than what we have.

Both of us had forgotten the details of what we'd written, and smiled with appreciation that we had filled the obvious gap in our first vows. 'Cheersing forks' is a given before every meal. Of course, this would have to be in the vows which uphold our marriage. This habit, which was born at our first meal together, represents how we twist the cultural norms to fit exactly how we want to live life. Cheersing forks is our way of life.

Chocolate in hand, we look to each other to start writing our latest vows, the second addendum. It feels comfortable to keep our 2020 vows concise, summing up what we love about our life together.

May our next five years together continue to be full of love, growth, happy times and good food.

Done.

This year, the plan was to go to Las Vegas and get married by 'Elvis'. I have a thing for Elvis. My dad has a great voice and does a mean Elvis impersonation. Now, anything Elvis is a total heartstring for me. The plan was to hire a convertible Cadillac, obviously, and get married at a drive-through wedding chapel, most likely with me wearing a tiara. With Covid-19 in full swing, however, Australia's borders are closed to overseas travel, with sporadic interstate border closures as well, so we've opted for a wedding closer to home. This year, we will return to our original wedding venue at Bilgola Beach.

Lucy arrives at our place at one o'clock. My 'little sister' from the mentoring program all those years ago is now twenty-one-years-old and fully entrenched as a member of our family. Today, she is our celebrant for the occasion. The three of us head north, driving up the beaches to Bilgola. I'm in my original wedding dress, which is mostly pale blue with a brown-tinged hem from spending a whole day dragging along the ground ten years ago. Joel dressed more casually today, rather than wearing his white-frilled Captain Jack Sparrow get-up which still hangs in the bag from the laundromat.

There are only a few other people on the beach today. One couple is having a romantic picnic, and we watch the man proposing to his girlfriend as we walk by. We continue up toward the sand dunes where Joel and I had a lot of our photos taken the first time around. The three of us stand in the sand, a little barefoot triad. The sky is overcast, there's a cool breeze coming straight off the ocean, and it feels like this moment is ours all over again. Lucy holds a beautiful ceremony, giving an unexpected speech reaffirming the love and family tie that has grown between us all, then reads our three sets of vows out loud so Joel and I can repeat them back to each other.

We stay for some photos before walking back along the beach, reminiscing, and telling Lucy all about it. Arriving back home, the first thing we do is wake Kitty up for a group hug. This is my family of four. My husband, Lucy, who I lovingly refer to as our second-hand daughter, and a furry cat who shits himself. My family make-up is not per the brochure, and that no longer feels like a good thing or a bad thing. It simply feels like *my* thing.

The Dance Floor

ood and *bad*. I grew up understanding these words to be mutually exclusive. This no longer feels like the truth. Admittedly, when we experience something that we don't like, we judge it accordingly. We deem the experience to be negative, and guard this opinion, rallying others who will confirm that it was, in fact, bad.

But then I come back to Wendy, playing. She loves this game. To Wendy, each move has a kind of poetry. Regardless of our judgement of something as good or bad, she sees the beautiful, underlying union of all pieces as they work together to create the game as we know it. It's a dance. It's eight billion perfect actions, all taking place synchronously on this dance floor. Each of us gliding around each other, seamlessly, fluidly. It's one lego piece twirling his partner, who then pivots and returns into his arms. Another piece spins off, making a graceful exit from the dance floor. A new lego piece steps up and is led by the hand of another into the gap which awaits their intertwined moves. Every piece has its place. It is elegance. This is a dance that has been choreographed with nothing but love.

The idea of love being the ultimate choreographer of all life experiences is not a new idea. In a letter rumoured to have been written by Albert Einstein, there is a wonderful explanation that offers a language for understanding the force that underpins all of life. In part, the unknown author wrote:

> "There is an extremely powerful force that, so far, science has not found a formal explanation to. It is a force that includes and governs all others and is even behind any phenomenon operating in the universe and has not yet been identified by us. This universal force is LOVE. This force explains everything and gives meaning to life. This is the variable that we have ignored for too long, maybe because we are afraid of love because it is the only energy in the universe that man has not learned to drive at will."

The whole movement of this game of life is run on love, by love and is love. This is what Wendy represents—the universal force. She is a metaphor for love itself. There is no play on this game board of life which is not, at its essence, moved by the force of love. Our limited minds cannot always see or hold onto this reality. We automatically revert to seeing through lego eyes and thinking with a lego brain.

Yet, if we can glimpse the broader view more and more, and hold focus on this view for longer periods of time, then we may just recognise this underlying love which permeates everything. In this space, we can feel the unity between us, beyond the stories of what 'she did', 'he said' or what happened—the view from above transcends all of that. It is to see the magnificence that is the entirety of the show.

No matter what our individual experiences are, we have the capacity to feel into a space beyond our limited perceptions to gain a broader perspective from the Vantage Point. From here, we can seek to find the silver lining to each so-called bad experience and appreciate its place in our life. We make the unconscious positives conscious. Only then can we find that love exists, even in our darker moments.

And if we find good in something we previously declared as bad, do we still label it as bad? It may have been an unpleasant experience. It may have been deeply upsetting, physically challenging, intensely emotional or mentally challenging. It may have been the hardest thing we ever lived through. Yet, if we can find the benefits born from it, then perhaps we can no longer refer to it as 'bad'. It may have uprooted life as we knew it, yet this experience was orchestrated by the same underlying force of love which permeates every experience on the board. Each play is setting up and allowing the next move to take place.

There is no bad. There are limited perceptions. There are no bad people. There are people. There are no bad events. There are events. There are many labels we can place on things, and we will continue to do so as an automatic lego response to life. Our lego brains are designed to keep us functioning as lego—for the good of the game. These brains are wired with a survival mechanism to judge every moment to decipher whether we are safe or in danger. We judge each person and experience as an instinctive self-protection strategy. Perceptions are instantaneous.

It is therefore only after our initial, knee-jerk reaction that we can gently guide ourselves to the Vantage Point. With self-care and a strong will, we draw our focus from our consuming emotions and judgements to see things from a broader perspective. We look for the beauty in each play. We look at the moves which took place after a 'bad' experience to see which moves were only possible *because* of it. If the whole game is progressing forward, *and we are the whole game*, then we have the capacity to find, acknowledge and feel this progression within ourselves, every time.

Two Lumpy Messengers

I am officially one year into writing this book. That is, since its inception *as a book*, with a publishing goal in mind. Leading up to that pivotal decision, I had already been writing material for this book for many years. Churned up thoughts and emotions led me to my keyboard again and again as I journalled about my experience trying to fall pregnant, as shared in my opening chapters. Really though, this habit of writing started to become ingrained in me when I was young. I wrote stories as a young girl. In my teenage years, I began writing poems. Throughout the tumultuous period which teen years can often be, expressing all I felt in words was an invaluable outlet. In my early twenties, poetry morphed into song writing, and occasionally I'd share these songs on 'open mic night' at pubs and boutique bars. There is a line from a song I wrote which has hit home in more ways than one since that time: *With my right hand on my heart and my left hand on my future, I fall into sleep.*

I was being quite literal at the time I wrote that line. I would go to sleep at night lying on my back, with my right hand over my heart and my left hand resting over my lower belly—my womb. Over the years, I have often revisited that lyric, fascinated by the way life unfolded. I thought my womb was promising a baby in my future. I understand now that this was a false interpretation. It never promised me a baby. It promised a future. And although this womb lying dormant under my left hand did not produce the future I anticipated, it was, without doubt, this womb and all it represented which deeply carved out my life's direction and shaped my future. This womb, in perfect accordance with the lyric, held its promise.

It was the first part of the lyric, however, which brought me out of a deep sleep last night. Sometime in the middle of the night, I woke up in this familiar position with my right hand on my heart and left hand on my future. Something felt new and unfamiliar. The fingers of my right hand were resting over two lumps in my left breast. First my brother, now me. It's turning out to be a lumpy year.

I lay there wondering whether I should tell Joel in the morning or wait until after a doctor's appointment when I had more information. I married a worrier. Any time I have anything beyond a common cold, he moves into a wee panic. He occasionally tells me that he's planning to die before me because he doesn't think he'll be able to handle the loss of me. Although, he also says this about our cat . . . hmmm.

I wake in the morning and, just as he does every morning, Joel asks me how I slept.

"It was interesting. I found two lumps in my breast." It just came out.

"You're going straight to the doctor today to get them checked out."

"Yep. And either they're nothing, or I get them cut out and deal with what may come. Maybe I'll need a double mastectomy and then I can get new boobs that will be forever perky."

"If you're getting new boobs, I get to choose them."

We both giggle at this last comment, making light of a new topic which may or may not turn into something serious. The most important thing is to keep it real, stay in the present, be practical, and then move through all necessary steps to bring the body back to health. This means not only taking these lumps to meet a doctor, but also embarking on an inward journey to investigate any emotional reason for manifesting them in the first place. Our bodies are loyally communicative. I have a firm belief that all symptoms are feedback from our body to our conscious awareness, telling us that something is awry in there. Something is unresolved, un-acknowledged or unloved. Our bodies let us know what's going on in the most subtle ways, increasing the volume, bit by bit, until we finally hear their announcement. The first step is to simply acknowledge the way they communicate. This is via what we refer to as 'symptoms'. Then we need to decode the message, and go inward to become aware of the cause. Was it environmental or emotional? If we can determine whether change is required in our external environment or within our state of mind, then we can truly acknowledge *and respond* to the message.

I book the doctor's appointment and let the topic rest until then.

As the evening falls, I arrive at the yoga studio and welcome people into the class. One yogi pauses at the door and asks me how I am. The moment I open my mouth to answer, I feel a rush of all-encompassing appreciation for my body's wisdom and its feedback system. This body is a perfectly functioning meaty intelligence which tells me as soon as something is out of balance. It evolved to keep balance and order, and it tells me straight away when something is out of line. That is an extremely healthy and optimally functioning system. In that split second, my response is very clear.

"I am really well, thank you."

Feeling very calm and quite 'matter of fact' about the whole thing, I roll with the process of first seeing the doctor, and then having the recommended ultrasound and mammogram. The doctor informs me there are in fact seven lumps, not two, many of them in my right breast. The right breast... it's the unattended side. As per the song lyrics, I fall asleep with my hand resting over my heart—more toward the left—so my right side just doesn't get as much attention as the left. The doctor loosely assures me that these lumps are all benign and suggests that my self examinations ramp up a few notches.

A brattish voice within surprised me with a sideways comment in response to the benign results,

"Well, that's not going to be very interesting for my book!"

By the time this sentiment was picked up by my brain, some other part of me, which is far more mature, abruptly sat upright and said,

"Be careful what you wish for, Sherrie Laryse."

Good point. Noted. Thank you.

In the meantime, I know a new part of my journey is about to begin. I am making the assumption that these cysts have not come about as a result of my external environment. I feel confident that my outer world is a healthy place. This redirects my attention toward my internal environment—embarking on a whole new investigation about what is out of balance, what is unloved, what my inner conflict may be. What is out of alignment that my body is calling my attention to? I hear the call. Yes, I'm onto it, thank you for letting me know.

Wendy's Funny Game

I call my dad today and the conversation starts with light chit chat, as it always does. I ask him how his dog is doing and there is a pause, then a broken reply that Tommy isn't doing so well, and they'll probably have to make 'the call' tomorrow. Tommy is old. He's fifteen, and he has tumours in his lungs. And, as of a couple of days ago, he has stopped eating.

I feel comfortable, albeit sad, in thinking that when an animal is old, has had a good life and is ready to go, then they're ready to go. I feel comfortable with the timing of this little four-legged lego piece being removed from the game. I also accept that it's easier for me to be comfortable with a loss when it's at arm's length.

At the same time, I feel a strong sense of unity within me, a unity with all of life. I see Tommy's life as analogous to one arm of an octopus. This one arm was a beautiful part of our existence, and now will leave us, but the body of the octopus remains. It lives on. Life lives on. Tommy's essence remains a part of the Whole.

All the while I try to be there for my dad, as best I can, over the phone. The biggest challenge is hearing him upset. I can hold my husband when he's sad, I can hold my brother, I can be there for my mum and for any friend, but my dad . . . On those rare occasions when I see my dad upset, I crumble. I hurt for his hurting, and I'm deeply sad that he is sad. I try to come back to the concept of Wendy to draw me out of this lego wormhole and back up to the Vantage Point where I can see more clearly. I need to take in this grand view and appreciate the beauty of every experience—and to be able to support my dad—but my lego-ness prevails. I wipe my tears and finish the phone call amidst these long silences while we're both trying to hold it together.

Wendy. Wendy. I try to get back to the Vantage Point.

This fear of loss sometimes feels insurmountable. It may be the loss of things we are attached to; be it our pets, people, money, jobs, all sorts of things. We humans do not usually fare well when something we're attached to is taken away from us. In my case, I recognise that it's the loss of my dad's happy, joking demeanour that I grieve. My dad is a comedian—not professionally, he was simply born funny. These rare moments where I witness him unable to find the humorous side of life brings up an innate fear of losing the dad I know.

A new day. A big day. As of today, Tommy's body rests under the soil until it will become a part of the earth again.

I remind myself, *nothing is ever missing*. Wendy is playing every role. Wendy *is* every role. She moves pieces on and off the board as the game progresses, but all pieces are herself. There is no difference. *Nothing ever dies*.

My cousin Corinne put it beautifully:

> "We're so used to recognising things with our eyes, that we feel they're not there as soon as we can't see them."

Lego eyes. We do have the capacity to see from the Vantage Point. Thanks to gravity, however, we return all too quickly to the default view at ground level.

It's now been three days since Tommy's body died. I spoke with my mum today and her experience paralleled my own. It wasn't Tommy's passing which upset her. She was sad, but at peace with that fact. What tore at her heart was seeing my dad upset. I hadn't realised before today what a patriarchal rock he is in our family. He has always been a very loving dad and a very fun dad. Growing up, he would make me feel like I was the most important and influential person in his world. Maybe because of this, he has always allowed me to feel like we were equals. He has never pulled rank over me or done anything in a domineering way. Fatherly guidance and gentle discipline, but there's nothing heavy handed in his nature*. He has always been the one bringing laughs to the table. When he and I get together, 'normal' goes sideways and almost everything is funny. My mum reckons that when I am within a kilometre from their house, my dad's degree of craziness begins to rise. Likewise, my husband tells me I become a lunatic approaching their house, just in anticipation of being with my dad. My dad taught me how to be happy in life, with life, no matter what. He raised me to be grateful for what we have—an "attitude of gratitude", he would say with an American accent. None of us are familiar with him faltering and losing his naturally upbeat persona. And it seems that neither my mum nor myself were prepared for how to handle it.

I find it such an interesting experiment, this whole 'life' thing. Rich emotions, expectations of what it *should* be, how we *should* feel, what we deem to be acceptable and what we shun. We seem to shun loss—at least, in the western culture in which I have been raised. Loss of a loved one and, as it turns out, even the loss of a specific trait in a loved one. Loss of familiarity. Loss of what we want. Loss of happiness. Loss of who we want. *Funny game, Wendy.* It matters not to her. She's wreaking havoc in one area, while flying butterflies and bluebirds in a clear sky over another. She has some lego pieces laughing so hard, their belly muscles are aching, while other lego pieces mourn, hurt, cry and die.

When they're all Wendy, it's all the same. Individuality is a human construct—lego ideology. Wendy holds all the strings, all the accents, and choreographs the scenes played with all the emotions, moment to moment. Wendy is holding the little lego piece who looks like my dad and portraying sadness in his body language and his words. She lowers his head and lets his heart temporarily droop with weight. I know that, at the same time, she's holding another lego piece and dramatically bouncing it up and down in some sort of joyous epiphany. Both roles are played. All roles *are* Wendy. I keep reminding myself, *nothing is missing, nothing is separate.*

---

* In *my* perception, I do not experience anything heavy-handed or strict about my dad's nature. He is gentle and light-hearted. Yet, if I consider that nothing is missing, then *nothing is missing*. This trait in my dad will also be present within him. It will show up somewhere in his personality in order for him to be whole—and he is whole. Even as I sit here at my computer on a Sunday morning, I can sense his life, his wholeness. I feel my dad's presence and all of who he is with the same realness as I feel my own breath. The ephemeral nature of it, yet almost tangible in the way the breath impacts and moves my physical body, proving its existence as undeniable.

Attachment

We celebrated my dad's seventieth birthday this weekend. It was warming to be with him and hug him in person, in the wake of losing Tommy. Amongst the *happy birthday* cheers, there were jibes about our surprise that my dad has made it this far at all. Given his lack of regard for self-preservation, along with his accident-prone nature, I am deeply thankful, and outright amazed, that my dad has lived to be this age—and a really healthy version at that! Perhaps amplified by my underlying morbid tendencies, I was cherishing each moment shared with him that day.

Other seventy-year-olds I've met along the way have whined and told me, "Don't get old, Sherrie, it's awful." These joking remarks, although said in a light-hearted fashion, come across with a degree of genuineness—perhaps a sense of disappointment that our bodies break down as they age. To avoid this situation, however, is to die young since we cannot alter the biological changes which naturally age our body over time. We could consider it an honour to live to an old age. That time of life is a gift which not everybody is granted.

And what is this obsession we have with thinking everything must be rosy all the time or it's not worth it? *I must always look good, I must always be healthy, fit and perfectly able. I must never feel pain, never have ailments, never have down days.* It seems there is an expectation that we should *always* be happy and able. Period.

What if life is simply an opportunity to embrace *all* of our phases? To embrace all of our experiences and the emotions that come with them, purely to experience the richness of life. Can we welcome our whole array of emotions, without wishing some of them away? Emotions are transient as it is. Could we find a way to welcome each one as it temporarily arises? Our emotions may arise as the result of an experience, but our emotions are not that experience. They are not the story; they are our response to the story. They're ours. Would it be possible to greet this part of ourselves with an inner smile, to accept it as part of our human experience? We can smile toward the feeling of happiness, smile at love, peacefulness, and satisfaction. We can easily smile at the emotions that we enjoy feeling. But can we find a way to internally smile at those emotions that are never smiled at? Or are we so attached to the idea of a one-sided, positive-only existence that we prefer to reject all other parts of ourselves? Buddhism teaches that attachment is the cause of our suffering. To my knowledge, this concept infers that attachment to *anything* causes suffering. Nothing is permanent—emotions, comfort, people's bodies, physical mobility—they all come and go throughout our life, constantly changing. Yet, all the while, we remain unchanging. Your body has changed, your thoughts have changed, and your emotions have cycled through nine million expressions; all is constantly changing. Yet, you are still you.

You are the unchanging aspect of your individual experience. The Wendy factor behind each of us is unchanging throughout the game. We are each a part of the Whole, having individual experiences at the lego level. We are allowed to feel down, as a part of our rich lego experience. We are allowed to feel pain. It does not become 'who we are' unless we choose to take it on as a part of our persona. It is merely physical sensation that forms a part of our experience. To quote a famous Buddhist teaching, "Pain is certain. Suffering is optional."

I say this knowing that when I injured my back and it was painful and awkward for a year, I felt quite deflated about it. I was truly attached to the idea of my body as healthy and flexible. It can feel very disempowering when the body we rely on defies us and dares to limit our experiences. It can feel disempowering to go from doctor to doctor, specialist to specialist, unable to find answers and relief. It can leave us feeling very vulnerable and at the mercy of this body we're in.

So, I contemplate the Vantage Point. I bring my thinking back to who we really are. Is it okay to experience pain? Sure. Do we like it? Generally speaking, absolutely not. Does it change who we are? Nope. Does it impact our human experience? Absolutely—although we get to choose *how*.

As Above, So Below

When astronauts first left earth, space bound, they turned to look back on our planet from afar. It was the first time the earth had been seen from a greater viewpoint, and it is said that this awakening view back toward earth was more impactful and significant than actually being in space or walking on the moon. Astronaut and space philosopher Frank White termed this deep shift in perspective "The Overview Effect", and described it as a recognition of the unified whole, without borders or boundaries between us.

The perspective with which we view life dictates whether we see ourselves as separate from each other, or as part of this unified whole.

There is a phrase I like, 'As above, so below', which originally appeared in a Hermetic text. The concept is said to have influenced Christianity which is where I first came across it. It simply states that what is above (some call it Heaven) is the same as what is below (us!). I find the phrase helpful to conceptualise the uniformity that exists between these two worlds—between macrocosm and microcosm. And while we can only speculate about what is above, if I apply the phrase as a framework, I can unpack what we do know to help me understand what we don't know. To start, I can investigate human biology at the microscopic size. I can home in on an individual cell, considering it from both above and below the cell membrane. Then I can incrementally draw my focus outward to repeat the process for larger and larger body parts. In doing this, I may recognise a pattern that traverses all we know about our internal world. If I find this pattern is preserved across all we know, all which happens *below*, then perhaps this pattern can be extrapolated to understand *above*.

I start by considering that our bodies are made up of trillions of individual cells. Within the cell are tiny little individual organs called organelles. Each of these organelles have certain characteristics that distinguish them[*]. They have their own functions to perform and their own goals in life. From this perspective, below the surface of the cell, each organelle recognises itself as separate from other organelles. From above, from the perspective of the cell, they are not separate at all. They are all another part of that same cell. They each make up the Whole.

Broadening my focus to outside the cell, I can see that

each cell's membrane defines it from other cells and gives it individuality. Each cell has its own functions, its own goals, and forms relationships with other cells. As a cell's external environment changes, it responds accordingly, constantly aiming to adapt as it moves through different stages of its life. I recognise how strongly we resemble the life of individual cells; sometimes feeling battered by ill health, sometimes being nourished in the perfect environment. And then, when it is time, death comes to all cells as part of the constant evolution of life and death within. In many ways, the internal world of our bodies parallels our external world as we perceive it. As above, so below.

And while each cell may perceive itself as separate from other cells, the 'above' perspective from each of our organs allows the organ to recognise these cells as itself. All cells make up the Whole. In the same vein, the organ knows itself to be separate from other organs. It has its own functions, its own goals, and has relationships with other organs. From the organ's perspective, it is separate and individual. And yet, each organ is a part of one whole physical body. They all make up the Whole.

Broadening my focus, I consider the perspective from our level of awareness. We know ourselves as separate from other people. The physical boundary of my skin, which contains everything that I am, proves I am not you, and vice versa. You and I perform different functions, have our own goals in life, and form relationships with different people.

The pattern emerges. From each perspective—the

organelle, the cell, the organ and our own—we believe ourselves to be separate and individual because we sense our external boundary. It is only by viewing each part from a broader perspective, that we recognise each individual part as just a part of the Whole. Identifying as separate versus being a part of the same One, therefore, seems to be a matter of which perspective we take.

Continuing to enlarge my perspective, I can appreciate how people identify as separate nationalities, commonly defined by the piece of land they took their first breath on. Yet, from the view above, there are no differences. There are no boundaries. This is *The Overview Effect* that astronauts experience. Unity among all humans on earth is obvious.

This pattern that is upheld suggests that separateness is merely a limited perspective. Humans perceive separateness. The pattern suggests that a broader perspective would allow us to perceive ourselves as One.

Preserving this pattern, we can consider the view from Wendy's Vantage Point. Wendy knows humanity is all her—without boundaries or borders. All parts—the earth, the clouds, the rain, the plants and animals—these 'individual' parts simply make up the Whole.

At the 'below' (lego) level, there is a sense of individuality, separation, life, and death. From the 'above' level, the sum of all apparent individuals is recognised as the Whole.

As above, so below. It is only the perspective we take which dictates our perception of individuality versus unity.

* Every year or so, I watch an animation called *The Inner Life of the Cell*, created by XVIVO, on YouTube (there is both a narrated version and an instrumental version). And every time I do, my breath is taken away with my absolute awe for life. We barely acknowledge, let alone appreciate, the complex inner workings of the communication and relationships that go on at this microscopic level. There are whole communities living within you. There is a whole and complete world within each of your cells which make up your body: a community of individual components, living together, yet each living an existence *as individuals*.

This animation allows us to look at the microscopic activity within. It offers an insight into individuality at the level of the cell—even the individuality of the mitochondria and proteins within the cell! At the same time, because of our vantage point, we can simultaneously appreciate that the individual cells and their internal components are actually just part of the Whole.

Perfect As We Are

In my biology classes at university, we are currently studying the evolution of various human conditions. This week, we discussed aspects of mental health and the functional properties of each condition to determine its advantages, either to the individual or to the survival of our species. When we considered anxiety, a suggestion was put forward that each group of people needs someone on lookout with a heightened sensitivity to danger. A person who is anxious will more readily detect a potential threat, thereby allowing the group to be better prepared to protect themselves.

I was listening in class and contributing to the discussion, but my thoughts were engrossed in Wendy's game plan. I remain impressed at the set up and distribution of all traits across the players. *She thought of everything*. Every single lego piece on the board plays an essential role. Each person, with their unique set of characteristics and behaviours, influences those around them, collectively impacting the direction of the whole game.

The traits we have, and the apparent 'shortcomings' we may think we have, are all required to play our role. They're not flaws. Each one of us is essential to the Whole just as we are. The way we think, change our mind—or not—is important for the rest of society. Collectively, we are eight billion jigsaw puzzle pieces with each of us being the exact shape required to create the whole picture. We each make up the Whole *because* of the way we are.

In every dramatised, choreographed dance, somebody is required to spin, seemingly out of control, so another dancer may deliberately swoop in to be there and catch them, stabilising them. Whether you play the dancer who is out of control, or the dancer who swoops in, both roles are essential to create the show. Working together like that is what makes the movement of the show brilliant, beautiful and utterly inspiring.

We are each essential—exactly as we are. Each person is needed exactly as they are. It's perfect play.

You are playing your role of being you perfectly. *Thank you.* Just be you. You're perfect.

Thinking

You are whole. You are a representation of everything, in that, you *are* everything. You're in this body, looking unique and sounding unique, yet what you are made of has all the components of the whole thing. You are the apple seed which holds the apple tree within it. You are the seed which holds the whole universe—incidentally, as is the apple. You are everything. Everything is you. Collectively, we role play differences. We role play so effectively, invested into every aspect of the game, that all of our senses support every claim of individuality and *prove* just how different we are from one person to the next—and to the apple. Quite obviously, we are not an apple. Or are we?

It's *oneness*. The magnitude of the concept stirs up my head and summons many thoughts for fresh consideration.

I first consider the question of fate versus free will. Wendy plays this game and moves pieces around the board as she pleases. I guess that's more like fate. Yet, we *are* Wendy. We *are* the one who moves the pieces. We *are* the free will which dictates the fate. Suddenly the concepts of fate and free will seem too black and white on their own to account for the whole picture. Under this model of thinking, I can appreciate how both are true, simultaneously.

I think about reincarnation next. Reincarnation says that while a person's body will die, their individual soul will return at some future point in a new form. The same individual soul, moving in a rhythm of lego player on, lego player off, lego player on, lego player off. This makes sense only if we deem ourselves to be individual. And, as lego, we do believe we are an individual because we experience full sensory awareness of our body's physical boundaries. We have our own personality, and we have our own memories. We are definitely individual—*at the level of the game*. Yet beyond our plastic lego-ness, there is no individuality. We are all Wendy at source. One Wendy playing every role.

So, I consider karma. Do our past actions, good or bad, flavour the experiences of our future? I think it through step by step. Our future is created by our current actions. Our current actions are in response to our perception of reality. Our perception of reality is based on past experiences and the judgements we made about those experiences. Abbreviated, our future is created by our past. In these terms, the concept of karma is indisputable.

If our future is created by our actions which are dictated by our perceptions, could this mean that our perceptions are the pivotal piece in understanding karma? Should we be focusing on balancing our perceptions if the aim is to balance our karma?

Ram Dass once said, "Everything in your life is there as a vehicle for your transformation. Use it!" This line of thinking has allowed me to find value in my undesirable experiences and therefore balance my perceptions about those experiences. John Demartini says, "Anything you can't say thank you for is baggage. Anything you can say thank you for is fuel." In my own experiences, finding gratitude for those things I initially perceived as baggage is what converted them into fuel. Perceptions are everything.

The placebo effect fascinates me as an example of perceptions creating reality. I find it wild that the health of many people will improve if they take a sugar pill, provided they believe the pill to be an active medication. Their health improves because they think it will. It seems we create our reality—on many levels—based on our expectations. So, is our own mind the merchant of our karma?

Recalling my goal-setting experience all those years ago: the corporate job I wanted to leave, the husband I wanted to meet, the $50,000 cash...Was it my karmic destiny to fulfil those three grandiose goals? Or did it happen because I was so filled with self-belief, inspired by what humans are capable of, that my expectations shifted deeply? By contrast, if I had been feeling sorry for myself, or frustrated by my unsatisfying work situation, I would likely have taken the alternate role offered to me or simply resigned, giving up any potential redundancy payout and the subsequent celebration where I met Joel. I would have missed all three goals had my mindset been different.

So, could our thinking, our judgements and perceptions all explain karma?

I first learned from Demartini about the blood flow around the brain, and how it changes depending on what we're doing or thinking. When we are doing something that aligns with our values, the blood flows to the front of our brain and we become more poised with clearer thinking. Our problem-solving skills increase, and we're better equipped to see life's obstacles as stepping-stones. Whereas if we feel guilty or angry about something, the blood flows toward the centre of the brain and further amplifies our perceptions of good versus bad. Our problem-solving skills decrease, obstacles become more difficult, and the way we perceive our reality changes. If this means we miss opportunities, lose relationships, health, or have some degree of misfortune, do we call it bad karma? Or is it the result of our own perceptions changing our brain's blood flow, which, in turn, changes the way we interpret—and respond to—the world?

To balance our perceptions, embracing both the negative and positive forces in our life is the catalyst for movement and progression. This is how we can find gratitude for our experiences. This is how we can appreciate life for what it is, as it is. One event played out opens into the next move of play. This is how we can use our experiences as fuel and as a vehicle for transformation.

This describes the private consultation work I do with people to help them find the positive perspectives of their negative experiences. It's designed to balance their thinking. I help people to connect the dots between an undesirable experience, and the desired outcomes born from it. Both positive and negative aspects work in unison as an inseparable pair. We can't change what happened, but we can change the way we think about it, and therefore the way we feel about it. Since 2016 when I started this work, I have not encountered one person who could not find the positives to their so-called negatives once we worked through the experience together. It's a perspective shift. And, ultimately, it's about letting go of rigid perspectives of good or bad, appreciating that both are at play, intertwined, always.

There is a beautiful Zen story about a farmer and his neighbour.

> The farmer's horse runs away one day, and the neighbour hears about this and says, "That's terrible news. That's too bad."
>
> The farmer responds, "Who knows?"
>
> The next day the horse returns, with an additional wild horse who followed. The neighbour says, "Now you have two horses! That's great news."

The farmer responds, "Who knows?"

The following day, the farmer's son takes the wild horse for a ride. The horse bucks and the son is thrown off, falling to the ground and breaking his leg. The neighbour says, "I'm sorry to hear that, that's very unfortunate."

The farmer responds, "Who knows?"

During this time, their country was in the middle of a war and the army was coming door to door to conscript young men. They knock on the farmer's door, looking for his son, yet, because of his broken leg, they leave the son at home. The neighbour says, "That was so fortunate!"

The farmer says, "Who knows?"

Was it his bad karma to lose his horse, or good karma to gain another? Do we call it bad karma that the son broke his leg or good karma that he avoided the frontline of a war? When each experience simply leads to the next, our judgement that an individual event be deemed good or bad (karma), could be completely contradicted by subsequent events.

It is to accept that we have the capacity to perceive either good or bad at the lego level. From a greater level of awareness, however, we can appreciate both aspects simultaneously and notice how they balance each other out. This is where positives and negatives come together to find equilibrium.

From a lego level of awareness, seeing a world full of good and bad, karma could be viewed as consequences made up of good and bad. If we are Wendy, however, recognising all beings as One, as love, as perfect pieces of the puzzle ... If we are here as Wendy in eight billion disguises, graciously welcoming all the ups and downs ... If we could welcome each experience anew, appreciating every necessary play of the game ... If we were unattached to thinking it must be a certain way, dictating what is good and desirable and what is otherwise, then maybe we could find some sense of peace in the perfection of it all, just as it is.

My thoughts whirl.

Undressing Wendy

I continue to let my mind roll in this new way around old thoughts. I revisit this idea of Wendy . . . This metaphor from within my meditation. Wendy is not a girl or even a person or any being with a personality. Yet I have continued to use her name and her existence as if she were a real, living, moving, thinking thing with a grander view of life and even an agenda. I've personified the concept of Wendy, referring to 'her' and how 'she' 'plays' her game. All of these terms anthropomorphise this abstract concept to simplify the notion for my own benefit, allowing me to more readily comprehend all the lessons I have been learning along the way. Yet, I may have also arrived at a point where it's time to unravel this metaphor and address—or indeed undress—the concept that is Wendy.

Wendy, whilst not a person, is also not a god of any

religion, nor an angel, not a spirit nor a higher being. Wendy is not a thinking thing. Wendy is a metaphor for the connection shared between all living things. Yet, not *just* the connection. Wendy is a metaphor for the base level element which makes up all things. Wendy is the metaphor for what makes up you, the apple, and all those things around you.

Throughout time, people have had their own names for what I've been calling Wendy. I really like the term *anima mundi*, which comes from Ancient Greek philosophy. This term, with its definition kneaded and refined by philosophers over time, refers to an intelligent and a vital force which permeates all of life. The words translate to "world soul". Anima mundi refers to harmony at the highest level. It is both the one and the many, and thus the intrinsic connection between all things.

From the same era, Aristotle referred to what he called *prime matter*. Prime matter is said to be devoid of form or specific quality, yet it has the capacity to become every single form in existence. It is claimed to be the substance which underlies all matter, all things which take form, and is therefore understood as pure potentiality.

Indian philosophy uses two Sanskrit terms, *Âkásha* and *Prana*. Together, they are the manifesting force which creates all things. Indian Yogi Swami Vivekananda offers a comprehensive explanation of which I've reproduced two paragraphs below[*]:

> According to the philosophers of India,

the whole universe is composed of two materials, one of which they call Âkâsha. It is the omnipresent, all-penetrating existence. Everything that has form, everything that is the result of combination, is evolved out of this Akasha. It is the Akasha that becomes the air, that becomes the liquids, that becomes the solids; it is the Akasha that becomes the sun, the earth, the moon, the stars, the comets; it is the Akasha that becomes the human body, the animal body, the plants, every form that we see, everything that can be sensed, everything that exists. It cannot be perceived; it is so subtle that it is beyond all ordinary perception; it can only be seen when it has become gross, has taken form. At the beginning of creation there is only this Akasha. At the end of the cycle the solids, the liquids, and the gases all melt into the Akasha again, and the next creation similarly proceeds out of this Akasha.

By what power is this Akasha manufactured into this universe? By the power of Prana. Just as Akasha is the infinite, omnipresent material of this universe, so is this Prana the infinite, omnipresent manifesting power of this universe. At the beginning and at the end of a cycle everything becomes Akasha, and all the forces that are in the universe resolve back into the Prana; in the next cycle, out of this

Prana is evolved everything that we call energy, everything that we call force. It is the Prana that is manifesting as motion; it is the Prana that is manifesting as gravitation, as magnetism. It is the Prana that is manifesting as the actions of the body, as the nerve currents, as thought force. From thought down to the lowest force, everything is but the manifestation of Prana. The sum total of all forces in the universe, mental or physical, when resolved back to their original state, is called Prana.

Italian philosopher Giordano Bruno believed that all aspects of life on earth, both animate and inanimate, were a seamless extension of a single unity which he called the Universal Soul. Universal Soul can be thought of as that which causes all things to come into form. Similar to the relationship between Akasha and Prana, Bruno proposed that the universe and all of life therein is a combination of Universal Soul and Universal Matter.

In modern times, scientific research has investigated this concept, called by its different names over time. Scientists have focused on finding the smallest common denominator of all matter. As technology improves, we advance our understanding piece by piece. The end goal of this quest is to find what is referred to as the Theory of Everything, a single theory which both unifies and explains all phenomena in the universe.

I bring my thoughts back to our bodies which are made of bones, muscles and organs. Over time, we came to understand that each of these parts is made of smaller components called cells. Inside cells, we found the organelles that I mentioned earlier. Science advanced and we found molecules and then atoms, once believed to be the smallest, 'indivisible' unit there was. As technology improved, so too did our knowledge as we found that atoms *were* divisible and were actually made up of protons, neutrons and electrons. Investigating further and we found quarks and, continuing further still, we arrive at the limits of current understanding where we find mostly space, in what is called Planck energy. To our current knowledge, humans are made up of predominantly energy. This incomprehensibly minute medium, called Planck level, is the smallest length science is aware of.

Modern philosopher Ervin Laszlo wrote a wild book called *Science and the Akashic Field,* where he explains the integrated Theory of Everything as a bridging of science and spirituality. His scientific explanation is as follows:

> "... the proto-consciousness that infuses the cosmos becomes localized and articulated as particles emerge from the vacuum and evolve into atoms and molecules. On life-bearing planets the atoms and molecules evolve into cells, organisms, and ecologies. Through them the consciousness that infuses the cosmos becomes more and more articulated. The human mind, associated with the remarkably evolved human brain, is the highest-level

articulation on this planet of the consciousness that, arising from the vacuum, pervades the cosmos."

These different explanations, from ancient Greek to Sanskrit, right through to modern science, all speak of the same phenomena. And it seems that the gap between the explanations is closing. Modern science is finding its way to meet these philosophies, which come in various descriptions, yet all have a common underlying theory. Wendy simply dangles on the outskirts as a meditated metaphor. Wendy represents the vast, uncontained, pure consciousness—pure potentiality. It is the connection that exists between all humans because it is what makes up every human. It makes up every other single thing which exists, that which we are also connected with and to. It is this base ingredient from which we come into form—our physical form which we identify as being.

Different slices of this metaphor, unfolding mid-meditation, can also be referenced with Sanskrit terms. The inherent belief we cling to, that our lego point of view *is* reality, is the illusion referred to as *māyā*. However, life—in my meditations, at least—is actually more of a game. Life is 'divine play', known in Sanskrit as *lila*. This *māyā* is ours to experience for what it is, for how we find it and for how we perceive it. This is the *lila*. This is the gift we have been graced with, form, the chance to be able to play this game at all. Every move, every play is born from Akasha and from Prana, prime matter, anima mundi and Universal Soul. It is the formless taking form to be able to experience any of this at all.

I bring my focus back to my own form. I observe my breath, and notice how it feels to have a body sitting in the position it's in right now. I am so much more than this body, yet it is through this body that I experience *everything*. My fingers hover above the keyboard, and I take a pause. Closing my eyes, I simply feel what it's like to be a breathing thing. I become aware of exactly how this body feels in this moment ... what it feels like to have a physical body at all.

This is the gift. Our bodies, in all their shapes, sizes and variations, is the present we were each given at birth. This wild gift. This manifestation of the formless into form.

* The full explanation can be read on Swami Vivekananda's website at www.ramakrishnavivekananda.info.

My Consummate Teacher

We're at home. Joel and I are laying back on our oversized couch, each with a cup of tea in hand, talking all things 'life.' I married a thinker, a philosophical type, so we always have something to talk about and different points of view to mull over together. We talk about karma, about reincarnation and about what makes up all things. Joel tells me about the urgency he feels to do certain things in life. He shares with me that he feels he's running out of time. Hearing these words come out of his mouth, his thoughts of leaving life prematurely, before he's ready ... something inside of me falls to the floor and weeps. I am used to having morbid thoughts about those I love. Ultimately, I find such thoughts helpful for enriching my relationships, and so I am comfortable with my mind's antics, even grateful. What I'm not ready for is

Joel reflecting these sentiments back to me about his own life. Such a dark shadow of sadness wraps around this potential reality and wipes the slate clean of all the philosophical thoughts I just had. On the outside, I keep a straight face. *Take a sip of tea. Maintain eye contact. Keep it together.*

As night comes, my senses are heightened to every moment we share—Joel brushing his teeth while I am in the shower; both having garbled, toothbrush-in-mouth, pre-bedtime conversations. I am acutely aware of every curl that reaches his shoulder, along with the grey hairs, growing in quantity, proving that we've already spent a good number of years together, ageing side by side. I am aware of his arms and the gentleness in his hands. I am acutely aware of his demeanour, and the beautifully raw vulnerability he shares with me by simply being himself, unguarded. I am aware of how much I love this human, overwhelmingly so.

Our Kitty already asleep on the end of the bed, we climb under the covers and find each other's bodies. A building film of sweat between us coerces me to break away from his shape—even though I don't want to. I find my side of the bed, allowing one foot to remain connected to his, cherishing this touch.

I fall straight into a dream. I'm at my old corporate job. My friends and colleagues are there, as is my old boss, Andy G. It's so good to see him again. We chat like old times and have some good banter. Partway through my dream, Andy G becomes unwell. I nurse him, and it feels good to have the opportunity to give back to this man who gifted my life with so much. Even in my dream, I recognise that this opportunity to spend time with Andy G is a gift granted to me only in this dreamscape. I know that when the dream is over, so too will be our time together. There is a recognition that this illusory dream state is analogous to how I perceive my reality of life with my lego point of view. In my dreamscape, I create a scene where different people are present and there are conversations, laughter, hugs … all the elements are present and played out and I feel it all. The scene may have been made up from thoughts in my head, yet the emotions arising from them are real, and their corresponding chemicals surge throughout my body. When I wake, I *feel* as if I've just connected again with my old friend.

I open my eyes in the morning and stare at the ceiling. I mentally run through the whole dream again, everything I can recall. The way I view my dream could be the way Wendy views her game—our lives. The conversations that took place in my dream were real to those in the dream, yet make-believe to the awake version of me who knew it was just a dream. My life, here and now, as I know it—the conversations, the laughs, the hugs, which are all real to me—could be equivalent to the collection of make-believe scenes to Wendy, who views her game from above.

As I lie here, I connect the dots. I recognise the deep sadness that will inevitably come if I lose Joel. I also recognise the broader perspective of all of this being *māyā*, an illusion; Wendy's dreamt up game playing out.

Joel and I are characters chosen by Wendy to portray a beautiful, deep, loving relationship. If it's all an illusion, then I can never really lose Joel. Again, I come back to the notion that nothing is ever missing. I can see Joel in my dreams as vividly as Wendy plays out his role in my life. Losing him would be the illusion, even though the chemical aspect of grief surging through my lego body would hold me under the guise that it is absolutely real.

I can't believe that Andy G came to me in my dreams to teach me yet another grounding lesson. I open-heartedly thank him, again, for the opportunity to experience major shifts in my world. Even after his death, he continues to support my growth.

Act Four, Scene Three

Today is my birthday. I am forty-three. I have not, as yet, had any hang ups about age and have always flatly refused to celebrate "Twenty-one again," as some people jokingly say when wishing others a happy birthday. I have embraced, loved and completely owned each new age I've reached. I've always felt that each birthday opened up a whole new world of opportunities and experiences accompanying that phase of life. Yet today … There's something different about today. I notice that I have dropped the 'only' from my age. For my previous ages, I felt I was 'only twenty-six' or 'only thirty-nine'. Just yesterday, I was 'only forty-two'. Today, though, I feel 'forty-three'. It seems that, overnight, my perspective has shifted.

I ponder what this may mean for my outlook and my resulting health. I wonder what will change in my body if I start acting like a forty-three-year-old. Does a forty-three-year-old even act in some particular way? Is there something that needs to shift as one approaches fifty? I'm not sure what I thought was meant to happen, or why forty-three feels like I crossed over some imaginary line.

Earlier in this book, I wrote that as long as we are experiencing a lego life, then we are confined by the limits of lego thinking, given this is how the game is played. Revisiting this concept now, I wonder whether *everybody* is confined to lego mentality, or maybe just some of us. Perhaps part of my lego role is to be confined within lego mentality, and that's why I think it's everybody's role because I view the world through *my* limited lego thinking. To say this applies to *all* lego pieces may just be small thinking on my part. I am merely lego, after all. It could simply be that my lego thinking limits my capacity to believe that others could escape these rules of play.

Perhaps another lego piece, such as Jesus or Yogananda, were able to secure a fixed position at the Vantage Point. They may have remained as physical lego pieces, while mentally living as Wendy, understanding the whole game through her eyes. I wonder if Yogananda ever felt forty-three. I wonder if he ever considered, even for a moment, the notion that his biological age signified something.

This question stays with me throughout the day. Are we all locked within our lego experience? Or are there some individuals who physically play the lego role, yet have perfectly clear vision through Wendy's eyes and never, ever falter in knowing who they are?

I go to bed, prop up my pillows and turn on my reading light. I've recently started a book my cousin leant me, *Mindfulness for Life*, by Dr Stephen McKenzie and Associate Professor Craig Hassed. At the end of chapter three, the authors include a timely quote from Albert Einstein:

> A human being is a part of the whole, called by us, 'Universe,' a part limited in time and space. He experiences himself, his thoughts and feelings as something separated from the rest—a kind of optical delusion of his consciousness. This delusion is a kind of prison for us, restricting us to our personal desires and to affection for a few persons nearest to us. Our task must be to free ourselves from this prison by widening our circle of compassion to embrace all living creatures and the whole of nature in its beauty. Nobody is able to achieve this completely, but striving for such achievement is in itself a part of the liberation and a foundation for inner security.

Apparently, Einstein and I are on the same page—in this regard at least. This quote tells me that he had a similar way of thinking. It seems that he glimpsed the game himself, from the Vantage Point, but also appreciated that we are here to experience ourselves as lego. Lego can temporarily view the entire game, yet, lego being lego, will always land back down into the core purpose of the game—with all the mental confinements that come with an individual lego experience. It's like a gravitational pull that we are all subject to on this planet.

The lego character I play is forty-three, and feels physical ageing coming on as part of this lego reality. I hope to embrace any physical changes as part of my experience as a lego piece in this game. We'll see how that decision holds up when I'm challenged!

Tapping In

Several weeks ago, Joel became unwell. We suspect his chronic fatigue has returned. While he's predominantly been sleeping, I've stepped up to make all the meals, do the shopping, the washing and run the errands. I do this whilst also running my consulting business, answering enquiries and placing orders for his photography business, finishing off my university assignments, studying for my exams, and preparing the yoga and meditation classes I teach each weeknight. I time all this around driving Joel to his various doctor appointments, sometimes up to five a week, as we try to find a way out of his symptoms. This experience gives me the tiniest glimpse of solo parenting, where you are wholly responsible for the health and happiness of another and have almost zero time for your own head space and own needs.

After doing this for seven weeks, I get to the pointy end of my busy schedule with a week of last-minute organising and arrangements to be made before I lead a weekend-long Yin Yoga & Meditation Retreat. On this retreat, I will host twelve people for a forty-nine-hour period. I need a lot of energy for this, and I do not want to go in feeling depleted. Right now, though, I'm feeling so tired. Other than my morning meditation, which has remained my saving grace, there is no head space in my day and my *I can do everything* mantra is showing fracture lines under the pressure.

This week, leading up to my retreat, Joel begins to improve. The more he improves, the more the built-up tension in me lets go—a little too abruptly—and I come crashing down. I feel absolutely spent and resign myself to rest for the remainder of the week. My body has that tired, vulnerable feeling where it feels susceptible to falling sick. I don't have time for *sick* right now, not this week, not with my retreat coming up. I'm nervous that my health won't hold up. I've poured so much energy into planning this retreat that I am disappointed to feel so utterly lacklustre as it finally approaches. Listening to my body, I cancel my evening classes for the week, and I simply rest.

This morning, in my meditation, I gained some perspective which dissolved my disappointment and made it all feel okay. In this meditation, I again became vividly aware of the bigger picture and the connection between us all. I temporarily moved outside of my lego mindset and truly felt a part of the whole thing, all of life. I felt 'tapped in' to all which exists and the basis of all of life—energy. It suddenly felt as if I could never truly be 'out of energy' as this is what literally makes up my whole body at the sub-atomic level of my cells. I *am* energy. Everything is. If I am alive, I cannot be *without* energy. In fact, I'm filled with it. So I have enough to hold this retreat. And even though my individual body feels depleted, I have a much bigger pool of energy to tap into to ensure this retreat happens as I intend. I don't need to solely rely on my own resources, when there is an unfathomable amount of energy which makes up this whole universal experience—and all of it is available, given that we are all a part of the same source. I suddenly feel completely supported, as if life has just been breathed into me and I am no longer expecting myself to breathe on my own. If I need extra energy to run this retreat and make it special for twelve people, then it's there for me.

I feel calm. I feel like it's all okay. I feel I am enough.

Whilst still seated on my bolster, I recall the meditation that has often been my go-to-practice over the years. In this practice, I visualise myself connecting downward into the core of the earth, and use this imagery to connect with the physical aspect of life, relating to people on a practical and tangible level. Then I send my focus upward, right out into space, with the intention of connecting with the bigger picture, to hold a broader, wiser perspective. I have a greater understanding of this meditation practice now that I have translated it into my current model of thinking. Connecting into the physical and tangible is to respect our lego experience as paramount. It acknowledges that we must be willing and open to live and connect in this way, because this *is* the game we're playing right now. It's the purpose of our whole experience. We are here as lego so that we can be lego and have a lego experience. Honouring that, let's be lego. I stay connected to the physical nature of all things.

Maintaining this feeling of downward connection, I then connect upward. I now recognise this place as Wendy's Vantage Point. This upward connection enables me to appreciate that this *is* a game of lego. We can play as lego while also holding an underlying knowledge that we are all one—and not confined to lego pieces at all.

Today, while this body I'm in feels tired, I hold this grander perspective vividly and draw on it all I need, because it is who I am.

Post Retreat Flow

Retreat done. I had everything I needed to nurture my retreat attendees exactly as intended. Not only did I have what I needed, but I've come home feeling utterly energised. I feel as if I'm floating, and yet, at the same time, fully charged and connected—earthed. Ideas come easily. I feel inspired. I feel a heightened sense of being on path, knowing that everything is happening as it's supposed to. It's a sense of being tapped into something greater, a perfect order in the world, where everything unfolds in front of me, making each next step obvious. For me, the feeling of inspiration is my compass to navigate through life, lighting up the next step on the path. The opportunity to run retreats and nurture people for a whole weekend fulfils the mothering need in me and wholeheartedly lights me up. This is what I want more of.

By Wednesday, my next retreat is already planned, with the venue and chef locked in. I've created a similar schedule to the previous retreat, which is essentially yoga, meditation, eat, meditation, yoga, eat, and repeat. I absolutely love the immersive experience of yoga teacher trainings, so I have replicated the same loaded schedule in the retreats I offer. The pace is relaxed, though the schedule is full. This next retreat will be in the winter, so I've added Saturday night Sangha around the fireplace. 'Sangha' is a Sanskrit word meaning 'community', a coming together where it is common to discuss yogic philosophy. I'm envisaging us draped over the couches with hot chocolates in hand, conversation flowing, hearts open, minds expanding.

Before announcing any news about the next retreat, one of the ladies from the weekend retreat emails to ask me to book a place for her on the next one "whenever that may be". My week continues to flow like this, with ease and order. Everything feels natural.

To draw out the retreat feeling, I bring one of the weekend practices into my Yin yoga classes for the week. I guide all the yogis into a meditation which blends Yoga Nidra meditation with Buddhism mindfulness techniques. In each pose, we drop a little bit deeper within. The first pose has us become aware of all we see, and tune in with all the sounds we can hear, exercising our ability to concentrate on just sight and sound. We begin the next pose with sight and sound, then also notice the taste in our mouth, any smells present as we inhale, the feeling of fabric on our skin, along with the temperature of the air on our exposed skin. We become completely familiar with our external environment.

Then we lower ourselves inward, noticing the physical sensations. Yin poses are ideal for this meditation practice as they tend to provide some fairly strong sensations which help to capture our attention. With our focus remaining inward, we then move our attention to areas of the body which hold the opposite sensations. We slowly check in on the whole body and the variety of sensations felt throughout.

Then we come to the breath. We notice the movement of air; the exchange going on between our external environment and our internal environment. We notice any thoughts that are present, either temporary thoughts passing through, or those which linger and give a theme to our current state of mind. We recognise the emotions present. We notice all of these things from the perspective of a curious enquirer—the one who investigates all the components of the present moment. And we become aware of the gap—the space that exists between the one who notices what is present and that which is present. We can be aware of thoughts, emotions, sensations, and we can switch our attention amongst them. We can notice our focus moving as we can notice all which changes. All the while, we can also become aware that we—the ones who observe all which changes—remain unchanging. We remain inwardly still, whilst noticing all the thoughts, coming and going. We hold the same witnessing position as Wendy (although I didn't refer to Wendy in class). We allow the gap between ourselves, as the observer of the experience, and all of the attributes of this present experience, to grow, allowing a little more spaciousness within. And we drop down into this spaciousness, into a sense of stillness. Similar to the ocean, where the waves on the surface may be wind-blown and choppy, we drop down beneath the surface activity into the calm, stillness below.

The last Yin pose we come into has everyone move through these meditation steps, beginning with sight and sound, and continuing until they reach a final place of stillness. Each person finds their own way there, at their own pace, proving to themselves that they can navigate their way here on their own. We rest here in our own inner place of peace and stillness, feeling a sense of spaciousness from all activity. To me, this is equivalent to hanging out with Wendy.

I drive home after class and unpack my bag. My iPad and my notebook of stick-figure class plans both go back onto the shelf above my desk. I'm buzzing, as I usually am after teaching at night. I am in the routine of doing a post-class meditation to help me to slow everything back down so I can fall asleep more easily. Tonight, I come into the same meditation I shared in class, as I've done so many times before.

In the quietude beneath the waves of everything sensory, emotional and mental which make up this moment, I settle into stillness, coming to a place within of complete spaciousness. I arrive here easily tonight. Rupturing this quiet space, I hear a man's voice from within my meditation. It's like gravel. It's low and gruff, broken, and he's yelling—at me. This man is livid. The bitterness coming through him is palpable.

I feel an initial wave of trepidation, immediately followed by the recognition that it is okay to stay here. It feels comfortable to simply be with whatever may happen next. I am curious why he is showing up in this deep, and supposedly the calmest, space within myself.

I stay for a while, watching, waiting, and the yelling soon stops. The man's anger seems to subside, yet his face remains poised for another angry outburst. I hold my position. The feeling of bitterness from him slowly fades. It feels like a big moment for this male presence simply to be seen and acknowledged—seen, without me turning my back and leaving. I feel the magnitude of me seeing him *and staying here*, making his presence welcomed and accepted. For a long while, we simply stay in each other's presence. It feels as if that's all we can do; yet it feels as if that is perfectly enough.

I come out of the meditation, not understanding what it meant, but comfortable with that, too. Time for bed.

It's morning. I wake. I grab my bolster. I set up for meditation. It doesn't take long to drop into the stillness within. The man is here. He's sitting on the ground, leaning his back up against a wall. He has a cigarette in one hand, head tilted upward with his lips pursed, watching the long, white cloud of smoke he exhales.

What the 'f' is going on in my psyche?

This questioning draws me out of the stillness that exists under thought. I am drawn back upward, and my mind remains quite chatty for the rest of the meditation. I'll go back tomorrow.

Sun up. Bolster laid out on the sheepskin rug. The cat settles himself on the bed next to me. It's meditation time. Time to meet the man. I breathe, I drop down, thought draws me back up again. Breathe. I settle my thoughts, slow my breath and aim on dropping back into my inner stillness. Problem: I am going there so I can see *him*. Knowing my aim, I get stuck in the cycle of trying to force something to happen. My thoughts continue chattering and hold me very superficially today, unable to slip beneath the mental noise. Each time I start to drop, I think. I come back up. There is no contact made today.

Sun up. Bolster down. Cat. Thoughts. Lots of them. My intention to visit the man again is the very thought which holds me back from entering the inner space where we meet.

Third failed attempt. I decide to rest the idea. I resign myself to the understanding that my thought to go back there will ensure I cannot get back to the place which exists under thought. I reassure myself with the notion that perhaps that first meeting was all that was required to acknowledge this inner part of me—to calm the anger. I let him rest there. Until we meet again, sir.

Act Four, Scene Three, Frame 22

I've been forty-three for all of twenty-two days now. Last week, I began noticing that it was taking me longer to read on screen. I found it was taking greater concentration to get through each sentence. When I think about it, I first noticed this change creeping in during my biology classes throughout the semester. During the tutorials, we often paused to read online articles individually, then came back together to share our opinion with the group. I felt significant pressure trying to read the articles in the allocated time. I recognised that, for some reason, I was struggling to concentrate on the words and take everything in as I normally would. Despite my underlying recognition of this, I dismissed it and didn't think too much about why.

Last weekend, while looking at my laptop (writing this book!), I covered one eye at a time and tried to read the words on the screen. The vision in my left eye was crystal clear. I've always felt that this eye had stronger vision. In the past, when I've looked into the mirror and stared into both of my eyes, it was my left eye which always seemed to penetrate a little more deeply, to see a little more clearly. The eyesight in my right eye, although still clear back then, has become a little blurry these days when looking at a computer screen.

Years ago, one of my older friends told me that as soon as you reach forty-years-old, your eyesight starts to deteriorate, and glasses become a part of life. I remember being annoyed that he mentioned this so matter-of-factly. Inwardly, I rejected his statement. I decided to prove him wrong. Every year beyond forty that I had crystal clear vision seemed like a little win in the secret game of *Me versus Stereotypical Ageing*. I told myself that as long as I processed my emotions and didn't view life through rose-tinted glasses or a veil of bitterness, then I would be able to see life clearly. I recognise now that this was an unrealistic theory. The obligatory acknowledgement of my deteriorating eyesight feels as though I am about to lose in my own secret game. It's not even about the glasses. It's about what I made glasses represent if *I* wore them—the loss of choice, and the loss of the power I believed I had over my experiences. It's the cringing feeling of succumbing to stereotypes, as if I'm living out a generalised expectation rather than creating my own personal experience.

Maybe it was these subtle changes in my eyesight which subconsciously influenced me to drop the 'only' from my stated age. The grey hair never bothered me. My mum tells me she had her first greys at twenty-one. This fact allowed me to completely sever the relationship between *grey* and *old*. Grey is now just another hair colour, amongst many. And although I dye my hair, I do embrace a few chunky grey streaks which I've left out of the dyeing process. As for the wrinkles, I've had smile lines since I was a teenager. I remember my initial embarrassment when people pointed out my wrinkles in high school, but I learned to embrace them as the badge of a happy life.

My eyesight, though . . . this feels different. I make the optometrist appointment and front up at the shop at ten o'clock to be tested.

Eye photos, glaucoma air-puff tests, miniature alphabet, dots, lines . . . all the regular vision tests rolled out. Immediately, the optometrist starts talking about which glasses, which lenses, and what happens next for people 'my age'. He may as well have had a team of cheerleaders waving pompoms to celebrate a win for *Stereotypical Ageing* while watching me slump into the losing seat. And he was so matter of fact about it all. I don't think he was aware of the raw nerve he was pressing with his insensitivity toward someone who had just lost a secret game she's been playing for three years and twenty-two days. In response to his lack of bedside manner, I realise that I have an inward (and thankfully, silent) *"fuck you"* tendency to anybody who tells me that my body is incapable of doing what is perfectly natural. This reflexive sentiment is extended to inanimate objects such as plastic pregnancy tests and optometrists alike.

I politely cut off his monologue about adding an anti-glare, anti-scratch film to my new glasses and ask him about eye exercises instead; anything corrective, rather than band-aiding the problem. There was a pause and a perplexed look. It was as if I were speaking a foreign language. This was followed by a resounding "No." Then I realised that I was having an eye test in a retail shop which sells prescription glasses. They're here to sell glasses. They are going to sell me glasses, not advise me to focus on something far away, then on something near, until the elasticity of my eye muscles regenerate. I remind myself that eyesight degeneration is normal. My reflex kicks into gear again as an inner voice scoffs at me with a *"Fuck normal"*.

I see-saw for a while, mentally and emotionally, whilst outwardly moving through the motions of choosing the frames and deciding on the anti-glare, anti-scratch option. I then proceed to feel genuinely disappointed when they tell me my band aids won't be ready for another three weeks.

I leave the shop realising that my decision to wholeheartedly embrace this new age, and all that comes with turning forty-three, lasted all of twenty-two days. That's okay. In three weeks, I'll see a little more clearly and will be in a better position to embrace what this age actually looks like.

It's been one week since my eye test, and I feel my sight is getting worse by the day. This may be real or in my head, I can't tell. Computer time is now limited to a maximum window of ninety minutes, followed by a substantial break. In one of my breaks today, I went to yoga. I was lying in a Yin pose, eyes closed, and pondering my eyesight. If I'm not seeing life clearly, literally, then which aspect am I blurring? *Which part of life am I choosing not to see clearly?* Very quickly, the most logical, practical—and bland—answer landed: the natural ageing process. For three years, I have been blurring reality, thinking I can conquer nature and manipulate its rhythms. Human life begins with birth then moves through growth, peak, decline and ends with death. Accidents, illness and the like may intercept this process and bring death about earlier. Should that not happen though, we need a contingency plan—a fail-proof plan to fall back on. That contingency is the nature of ageing. I get it. I was fighting for something that isn't available, going against the laws of nature, and blurring my vision by believing I could have sustained youth. Thank you to my right eye, I see this now, more clearly than ever.

Evaluating this whole transitional ageing experience with my new model of thinking, I would say that my left eye sees the world through Wendy's eyes. I've always noticed a different level of vision through this eye, as strange as this may sound. My right eye sees my environment at ground level, as a lego eye. For the path that I am on, I need both. I need to be able to see from Wendy's Vantage Point and take in a broader perspective of the world. I also need to function day-to-day, and see where I'm walking. I need to be able to see that someone is upset and respond at the lego level, rather than just seeing the situation through my left eye and telling them that it's all happening out of love. I need both sets of vision. It now makes sense to me that my right eye, the one anchored more in the lego experience, would be the first to physically decline, perfectly aligned with the natural cycle of lego life.

Full Circle

Joel and I pack the car with our overnight bags and snacks for the road. The passenger is always the DJ, and today I chose Xavier Rudd to accompany us out of the city and onto the highway. There is a warehouse a few hours south of Sydney that I want to visit. My cousin Corinne lives relatively close to where we're headed, and has kindly invited us to stay at her home. It will be amazing to catch up with Corinne and her family. The full download will need to wait until hot coffee and a big breakfast cook up tomorrow morning. Tonight, both Corinne and her husband are headed out to a Christmas party, and so Joel and I will spend the evening with their two daughters.

We arrive at their home in the afternoon and the girls show us their rooms, their drawings, their books, and talk about the latest conspiracy theories. Come evening, the four of us head out to the girls' favourite schnitzel restaurant for dinner. Joel quietly commented to me as we were leaving the restaurant, "We look like parents taking our daughters out for dinner." The thought truly hadn't occurred to me and even seemed a little random, if not irrelevant. Even so, I agreed, and we laughed it off as we walked out with 'our' girls.

Now that I'm revisiting this conversation, I can acknowledge my current headspace compared to where I was a few years ago, when walking into the public school to pick up my nephews. Back then, I was totally consumed by the thought (translation: desperation) of being a parent. I recall walking through the school gates trying to forge a feeling of normalcy, as if I did it every weekday. I was trying so hard to conjure up the feeling of what it might be like to be a parent. In that scenario, I was striving for an imagined reality where I could think like a parent, look like a parent and, most importantly, feel like a parent. I deeply desired for my life to be something other than what it was.

And now, a few years later, Joel's very valid comment passes straight through me without even touching the sides. I appreciate that the current state of mind I hold is just as temporary as any other, but for right now, it feels appropriate to honour the path I've walked and acknowledge how far I've come. I no longer feel the need to cling to an imaginary version of parenting as an avenue for feeling the experience. I find myself in a refreshing state of recognition that I am 100% a parent, in my own way. It feels like I've come full circle but, this time, I'm coming back around as a whole new version of me where I am already a mother. Whilst I continue to strive for more opportunities to mother, the point is, I already feel like a parent. I have satisfied this void within to a level where I no longer feel a void. It feels like my life is fulfilled. It feels like a purposeful life. It feels like a driven life—even led.

Today, right now, I feel grateful. I feel loved and I feel love. And I feel completely supported on my path.

On Path

This book has moved through a few iterations concerning its title. It started as *An Investigated Path*, representing my inner work to understand the capacity of humans beyond what we're taught. Then, sometime after the first few chapters, I changed it to *Trust*, which reflected how we can move through our challenges and find growth in the face of loss. This title spoke of my turning point where I felt held by a grander plan which was being laid out in front of me; a plan which was outside of my small mind. I felt that I was able to find reason in every twist and turn of my life. I recognised that all of my experiences "were *on* the way, not *in* the way", as Demartini puts it. I truly learned trust.

Next, I changed the title to *On Path*. This title continues to feel representative of the message—so far.

However, we'll see where it all goes and how the story continues to write itself, day by day. Yet, that in itself is the exact point. No matter where this book goes next, no matter where my life goes next, that *will* be the path that I am on. I will never be off path, regardless of whether my experiences make sense to me or meet my expectations. I am very familiar with this notion now. When I look back over the path I have walked, I walked it having zero idea where it would lead to next. I had a direction in mind, yet, despite my best laid plans, that is not where I ended up. And my intended direction didn't even include a big, grandiose goal . . . I just wanted to fall pregnant.

As life would have it, Wendy had a vision that she could see with perfect clarity and had a game plan to match. I was going to be a mum, alright. There was a way I needed to get there though, a specific path I needed to take.

My growing frustration in a corporate job inspired me to enrol into a particular weekend course which did two things. Firstly, it launched a long-term, insatiable quest for learning everything I could about human behaviour and the essence of life. Secondly, I believe, it connected me with a man I fell in love with and later married. Then, our inability to bear children heavily (if not purely) motivated this need to receive more knowledge, so I therefore had more to give others—teaching being a key component of mothering in my eyes. Born from this drive, came one of my favourite affirmations in respect and recognition of the full cycle of exchange: *The more I receive, the more I give. The more I give, the more I receive.* For me, this translates to receiving more knowledge to give more knowledge, and giving more knowledge means I receive more fulfilment. Connecting the dots . . . as long as I keep learning, I can keep teaching and, that way, fulfil this aspect of my motherhood.

Looking for more avenues to share what I learn, more avenues to mother, I join a heart-felt group of women who mentor teenage girls. At the same time, a new qualification allows me to start a consulting business to provide people with guidance for moving through and processing challenges in their life. This is me mothering, one on one. This is me helping each of my babes work through a difficult time in their life. This is me teaching people how to not only overcome challenge, but how to own this new paradigm of thinking so they may be empowered to process their experience and have the tools to move through future challenges. To me, this is the way I love to mother. I'm not about building dependent relationships with people who need to come back to see me every week. I teach people emotional intelligence—that is, how to process emotions. It is a technique which uses purely the mental faculties, because after all, it is our viewpoint of something, our perspectives, which dictate our emotional judgements about that experience. Our thoughts create our emotions, so it is our thoughts that I work with in order to create emotional independence in people.

Following the cookie crumbs further down my path, working with people one-on-one grew into working with groups of people in a yoga setting. Becoming more comfortable at the front of a yoga studio planted new seeds and, coupled with my quest for more knowledge, I later enrolled into yoga teacher training myself. I see yoga as a somatic way of helping people gain deep emotional release, as well as the aftermath of growth, which I have found the practice offers. It was this training, and my unexpected deep love for teaching it, which led me to the initial concept of writing a book—a book about yoga. That book led me to this book. This book led me to write, in far more detail than I would have otherwise, about my experiences moving through my friend's death.

Not only did this dictate a surprising direction in the book, but it also introduced me to the concept which I playfully refer to as Wendy, that which has literally changed my whole outlook and attitude since then. The more I delve into this 'construct' (belief, thought, concept—whatever the correct word is here), the more I am moved to see everybody else as me. This has completely turned my world around and impacted every way in which I relate to others—people I don't know and people I do know. People I like and people I don't like. When I can hold this theory of Wendy, that each of these people is me and I am them, my love for that person expands exponentially and my initial perspectives of this person or situation dissipates into nothing but love, and the kind of supportive curiosity you feel when wondering what a toddler is going to do next after they wobble and fall. When I see people as me, my heart opens to them. When my heart opens to them, I can let them in. I can love them in a way that I simply couldn't before. I can actually hold them in my heart, completely, and if this isn't mothering, I don't know what is.

This is my path.

While it hasn't always felt full of sunshine and butterflies, I genuinely appreciate that this is my path for a reason. Each experience paved the way for the next part . . . which paved the way for the next part . . . each step taking me forward on my path. There is a blog post on my website, which I wrote years ago, called "No Rain, No Flowers". It is this concept exactly. Sometimes we can perceive that the rainy times in our life are 'raining on our parade', but in truth, they are simply watering the flowers of our life so they may grow. We are never *off* path. The rain is an important part of our growth along that path, just as much as the sunny moments are.

We are never off path.

We may feel as if life is moving in an unplanned direction, yet who is to say that our initial dreamt-up plans would have taken us where we wanted to go? Who is to say we weren't meant to hold those initial plans simply as a bridge to these new plans? Who is to say that there isn't somewhere more ideal for us, if we only had the capacity to think so grandly about ourselves? Wendy really does have a much broader perspective from her Vantage Point. I'm going to go with her choices every time, whatever life brings.

All of our experiences are on the way, not in the

way. And while the immediate surprise of where my path goes may instigate a little tantrum in me initially, like turning forty-three and feeling the first unwanted signs of ageing, I choose to allow my emotional legoness to be just as alive in me as Wendy is. I choose both perspectives. I can recognise my wholeness, whilst I feel my shortcomings. I can question my experiences, whilst simultaneously knowing that I am on path. I can be lego, all the while recognising that I am also Wendy. Being human is to hold it all.

The End

I finished writing that last chapter and saved one copy on the hard drive, a backup file in the cloud, and put the computer to sleep. I deserved yoga.

On my walk to the local studio, it dawned on me that I had just written the last chapter of my book. Although unexpected, it definitely felt like closure. All along, I have felt as if this book was writing itself. Sometimes it was a sense that the words came through me, and I merely let my fingers move, freestyle, over the keyboard. At other times, I noticed my own conscious thinking was finding each word by word. While I have oscillated between both 'writing voices', I feel that this is the very essence of the book. It is that we *can* move between the two viewpoints in our experiences. We can see life from the Vantage Point and recognise the entirety of this grand plan, and we can also take the ground level perspective to appreciate the human experience. This book is a representation of that movement—the whole experience.

While I feel an initial wave of surprise, and perhaps hesitation, around my book coming to an end, I have learned to accept my experiences as they are. I may not like them, I may not initially agree with them, I may initially wish it were another way, but I accept them. I acknowledge all of the human emotions that are present, and allow them room to move and the opportunity to be felt. All the while, I have learned to trust—trust my path.

So, in that moment, walking to yoga and feeling into 'the end', there was a kind of numbness, or a lost feeling, as if I'd lost my ground. I walked in a slight daze, emotions swirling, whilst telling myself that I'd think about it more during the class and see how I felt afterwards.

Continuing further on my walk, attempting to push these strange feelings of goodbye to the back stalls so I could have some time to think, I imagined printing out my manuscript to give to my mum for Christmas. She would be the first person to read it. Christmas was just over a week away. It would be perfect.

This fleeting thought brought an increased level of certainty about the closure of the book, and immediately my eyes started welling up.

I arrived at yoga, walked quietly into the studio, gathered my props and unrolled my mat. I lay my body into the first pose, and I started to gently cry. I had anticipated a whole other emotion to be present in that moment when my book came to a natural close, but here I was silently crying.

I cried for the ending of something that has been giving me so much joy, so much fulfilment, and a far greater capacity to process thoughts and experiences in my own way. I cried for the ending of my opportunity to share wild meditations, without restriction, in a space which felt completely un-influenced and un-judged by outside opinions. I cried for what feels like the end of a relationship; this silent confidante to whom I unravel all of my deepest thoughts and inklings whilst they piece themselves together. I cried over the abrupt break up of an eight-year love affair, scribing my whole journey via this keyboard. I cried for my baby, recognising that it is all grown up and about to leave home.

I cried for the loss of ongoing conversations (albeit one-way), whenever I had a thought and wanted to sit down at my computer to shape it into words. I cried in fear of needing to act on the next step and what would come of my baby from here. I cried for the anti-climactic ending, this story so sneakily wrapping itself up with the undeniable recognition that I have come full circle. I had answers to my questions. It was over. I was sure I had been building up to a grand crescendo all this time. Although, at the same time, I was cautious about what that grand crescendo may have been—what my next dramatic gain or loss would be that I needed to work through in words worth sharing. This part of me sighs with relief that there's no great catastrophe to grow from and write through the process. And so, I cried over whether this book would be *enough*. I cried over the shortness of it, in comparison to the full-length version my imagination became attached to. I cried because I haven't yet worked out why there's a guy smoking cigarettes in my psyche, and, when I do, who do I tell? Tears slowly rolled down my cheeks all the way through class.

Nearing the end of class, the teacher shared a saying by Lao Tzu:

> "Be content with what you have. Rejoice in the way things are. When you realise that nothing is lacking, the whole world belongs to you."

Nothing is lacking. 'Wendy' is playing through me. I am actually Wendy under this Sherrie suit. Through living my path, I have come to know myself as whole, as everything—as the metaphorical Wendy. I have come to know myself as limitless, as all-encompassing and complete. I have come to understand myself beyond the limitations of my dermal boundaries, yet at the same time, acknowledging the absolute gift that this body is, *so* I may experience *any* of this. I have come to appreciate that my experience is perfect, just the way it is. I acknowledge that within this experience, the analogous lego experience, that my thinking capacity is generally small minded for day-to-day purposes. I acknowledge that, as a part of this lego experience.

I get angry, I laugh, I obsess, I hunger, I hurt, I dwell and I mourn. I fully embrace all of the temporary aspects of this lego life with all the joys and pains that come with it. I have come to know this as life—this is life—the oscillations between the profound insight of knowing who we really are, and utterly saturating ourselves with the human experience we are here to have. And, we are allowed both. We are allowed to fluctuate between both realities, both states of mind—the open expansiveness and the gravitational contraction. We are both. We can tap into either, and allow ourselves to experience both aspects willingly. All the while, we are also free to choose one of these viewpoints exclusively over the other.

The way you play this game of life is your path. Life unfolds the way it unfolds, with all its twists and turns. We each choose how we make sense of all these unfolding events, and it's this choice that dictates where we go next. This is what makes up our path – it's us. It's our perspectives, it's our decisions, it's our reactions. It's our way. *Our way* creates our way.

I wanted my path to be a mothering path. If I had raised my own children I would have, presumably, felt completely satisfied and poured all my focus into them. Yet, here I am, without little ones who look like me. Instead, I am focusing on sharing all of this with you. Through my words, I open my heart to you. I write this for you.

With gratitude...

First and foremost, my gratitude goes out to Joel, namely, for being Joel. His support for me writing this book made the whole process truly enjoyable. Some days, when I was tired and it seemed the stairs up to our front door were harder to climb than usual, he would either push me up from behind, or grab the waistline of my jeans and kind of pull me up. I'm not sure whether it was his helpful gesture that aided in lightening my mental load, or my own efforts to lift myself up, trying to beat the denim up the stairs in an attempt to escape the wedgie. Either way his support was real.

Thank you to my Mama, my role model. In addition to your unwavering and bottomless love and support, thank you for being the first guinea pig to read my manuscript in its rawest form and providing your wise and thoughtful feedback.

Thank you, Papa, for igniting my self belief. It has made me who I am and made my life what it is.

Thank you, John Demartini, firstly for your substantial influence on my thinking. Secondly, for your time, wisdom and talking me through human behaviour and your take on karma—your input felt like gold.

Thank you to all of my friends and family who have nourished my world with your time and conversation—and provided meat for my stories. Lucy (whose name has been changed for this book), you make my heart feel whole. Thank you to the neighbour up the road who thought it best to give away her cat—he changed my life.

Thank you to LEGO for kindly letting me use your name—confirming again that this book has no connection with the LEGO group, nor is it endorsed, sponsored by, any of it . . . all of it.

Thank you to my manuscript assessor, Heather Miller, for being the first professional eyeballs on a first-time author manuscript. I am very thankful for your insightful guidance, as well as your encouragement to share more of the personal details of my path.

To my American editor, my main editor, Kendra Langeteig, a huge thank you to you. You were so gentle with me! All of your feedback was so thorough, so considered, and was delivered with such care. I cannot thank you enough for helping me convert my pages of words into a book worth reading. And whilst some of my 'Australianisms' remain, and may bewilder a few people around the world, you did convince me to review many expressions which make perfect sense 'down under', yet absolutely no sense in any other English-speaking country! Mostly, thank you for meeting me where I was, at the very beginning of the author's road, and holding my hand while we worked on this book together. I am forever grateful.

Finally, to Lin Fong, my Australian editor. Your final coat of polish on my manuscript confirmed my readiness to share this story. Thank you for giving me the confidence to double down on some of those remaining Australianisms, making sure they were correctly aligned with our incorrect use of the English language :)

This book has certainly been a team effort. I am incredibly thankful to everybody who has co-parented this book with me.

With love and gratitude,

Sherrie

www.ingramcontent.com/pod-product-compliance
Lightning Source LLC
Chambersburg PA
CBHW020319010526
44107CB00054B/1909